DANCING IN BLOOD

DANCING
IN
BLOOD

Exposing the Gun Ban Lobby's
Playbook to Destroy Your Rights

Alan Gottlieb
Dave Workman

Merril Press
Bellevue, Washington

Dancing in Blood is published by
Merril Press, P.O. Box 1682, Bellevue, WA 98009.
www.merrilpress.com
Phone: 425-454-7009
Distributed to the book trade by
Midpoint Trade Books, 27 W. 20th Street, New York, N.Y. 10011
www.midpointtradebooks.com
Phone: 212-727-0190

FIRST EDITION

ISBN 978-0-936783-65-9

Library of Congress Control Number: 2014949507

PRINTED IN THE UNITED STATES OF AMERICA

DEDICATED TO ALL THE VICTIMS OF GUN CONTROL
WHO HAVE LOST THEIR LIVES OR LOVED ONES
TO POLICIES OF PUBLIC DISARMAMENT
AND THE POLITICS OF GUN CONTROL DEMAGOGUERY.

CONTENTS

CHAPTER 1

THERE REALLY IS A GUN CONTROL PLAYBOOK!

Following the tragic school shooting at Sandy Hook Elementary School in December 2012, the powerful and well-financed gun prohibition lobby, supported by such people as billionaire anti-gun advocate Michael Bloomberg, then still serving as mayor of New York, launched a massive multi-tiered campaign to push its political agenda back into the spotlight.

This was no ordinary effort, but a well-coordinated assault on the firearm civil rights affirmed and protected by the Second Amendment, dozens of state constitutions and two recent U.S. Supreme Court rulings. Gun control proponents had the right buzz words, and they knew how to ignite and appeal to public emotion. They were able to steer the conversation toward subject areas that had little or nothing to do with the heinous crime, but had everything to do with advancing a plethora of gun control measures that had been on their wish list for several years.

Gun control became once again a hot political topic, with conversations dominating the Sunday morning network news circuit. People representing the gun prohibition movement had their talking points and repeated them with each new appearance before the cameras.

Efforts were launched in several states to press for local gun control measures as it became evident that Congress was not going to rush the adoption of the anti-gun political agenda.

This was really nothing new, because gun prohibitionists have for years, tried to capitalize on every tragedy to push their agenda, regardless whether anything they have ever proposed as a legislative "fix" would have prevented the particular crime they were now exploiting.

Once again, to so many in the gun rights movement who have been on the front lines of the battle to stop legislative erosion of the Second

1

Amendment, this was the gun grabbers "dancing in blood." In some cases, their efforts became a disgusting spectacle of political crassness. Indeed, Bloomberg's first statement on the massacre was issued before the bodies of the victims had been removed from the school building.

This time around, however, to those defending firearm rights from this new onslaught, it seemed as though they were up against a well-choreographed team, working from a playbook.

And it turns out they were right.

For several years, the gun control movement had mounted attacks on Second Amendment rights from different angles and with various messages and strategies. Historically, the anti-gun-rights lobby maintained that the right to keep and bear arms was a collective right, meant only to allow the states to organize and maintain a militia. But in June 2008, with the U.S. Supreme Court's ruling in *District of Columbia* v. *Dick Anthony Heller*, that argument was turned upside down when the court said the Second Amendment protected an individual right to keep and bear arms that went far beyond service in a militia.

Followed two years later by the famous ruling in *McDonald* v. *City of Chicago* that incorporated the Second Amendment to the states via the Fourteenth Amendment, gun prohibitionists were stinging from two monumental losses. It did not mean they were throwing in the towel.

With Bloomberg willing to invest considerable amounts of his own capital in the effort, gun control proponents remained on the offensive, taking advantage of every high-profile shooting incident to insist that restrictions on law-abiding citizens were the only means of preventing such violent – albeit statistically rare – events.

Bloomberg's efforts went through a couple of evolutions. First there was Mayors Against Illegal Guns, which joined with another Bloomberg-funded group, Moms Demand Action Against Gun Violence in America in December 2013. Then in April 2014, Bloomberg – by now out of office and with plenty of time on his hands – announced a "re-structuring" of those groups into the "Everytown for Gun Safety" with a $50 million bank account.

But before we get too far ahead of ourselves, a look back at where the country was following the *McDonald* decision is important, because it finally appeared that anti-gun extremism had been derailed by the two high court gun rights victories.

Then came the mass shooting at the movie theater in Aurora, Colorado in July 2012. Dubbed the "Batman Massacre" because the shooting occurred during the late night premier of *The Dark Knight Rises*, the latest Batman movie, it rocked traditionally pro-gun Colorado. Yet instead of pointing fingers at the "no firearms" restriction imposed by the theater, which left moviegoers unarmed and defenseless against a madman who ignored the gun free zone signs, anti-gunners exploited the event.

Their efforts appeared to be running out of steam, but then came Sandy Hook, and the political landscape suddenly changed. Here was a vicious crime that victimized children. It did not matter that it happened in a gun free school zone, and that the killer got access to his weapons by murdering his mother, the legal owner of the guns. Nor did it matter that the firearms involved had all been legally obtained by her.

Seattle's then-anti-gun liberal Mayor Mike McGinn, who had joined Bloomberg's mayors' organization after taking office three years earlier, went to work in an effort to make some headlines and strike a blow for symbolism three thousand miles away. Seattle is a liberal bastion in Washington State, and some conservatives joke that the city is "only twenty minutes away from the United States in any direction."

McGinn and his staff organized a gun "buyback" effort in late January 2013, an event that even brought a caution from the head of the local gun control organization, Washington CeaseFire, that such efforts were essentially valueless in terms of preventing crime. They were good for a temporary headline, and that was about it.

But McGinn and his people were determined, and they pushed ahead, virtually ignoring the warning from CeaseFire's longtime board president, Ralph Fascitelli. McGinn wanted headlines and face time on television. He was heading into an election year and he wanted to appeal to his far-left base.

It was that event which led to the discovery of what soon became recognized as the "gun control playbook," an 80-page guide that detailed how gun control lobbying efforts should be conducted.

Clearly, this document was never meant for public dissemination. Its discovery was a matter of extraordinary luck. It was uncovered literally by accident.

Following the buyback effort, the Second Amendment Foundation (SAF) – the organization based in nearby Bellevue that was responsible for the *McDonald* federal lawsuit against the City of Chicago's handgun ban leading to the Supreme Court's 2010 Second Amendment ruling – sought all documents relating to the buyback under Washington's public records act.

A similar request went to King County Executive Dow Constantine's office, because he had supported the buyback, and SAF wanted to know to what extent the county may have devoted staff and resources to make the event happen.

Among the documents recovered from the county was a memo titled "Framing, Message and Language for Gun Violence Prevention." It had been produced by a research group based in Washington, D.C. and it was dated January 11, 2013. It appeared to offer advice on how to lobby the Washington Legislature on gun control measures.

When coauthor Alan Gottlieb did an internet search for the research firm, he stumbled upon an 80-page guide titled *Preventing Gun Violence Through Effective Messaging.* It had been inadvertently linked on the website of a religious organization that supported anti-violence efforts, but in a place one might not normally look. Its contents were stunning. Literally all of the gun prohibition movement's strategies, talking points and semantic sleights-of-hand were spelled out. There was advice on what to say and what not to say, when to speak and how to frame arguments. It contained all the buzz words, tips on how to milk a tragedy for emotional impact (i.e. "dance in blood") and how to spin a conversation away from embarrassing talking points.

Here in one reference guide were essentially all of the battle tactics in the national gun control campaign. When coauthor Dave Workman's calls to the authors of the document went unanswered, it was clear that Gottlieb had uncovered what might be considered "the mother lode" because they now had the "gun control playbook" and it was more than just a mythical document that might be alluded to with tongue-in-cheek. The "playbook" was real, and now gun rights advocates could study it.

More importantly, it was clear that information in the guide had already been used, and was being employed, in gun control efforts in Washington State, where SAF and the authors are headquartered.

Perhaps most important of all was the realization that this document had been intended for covert use. This was the "battle plan" for anti-gunners, and one can safely conclude they wanted it kept secret. As if to underscore that point, months later, at a gun control planning session in Seattle, copies of the guide were made available to the anti-gun activists who attended.

Disturbingly, *Preventing Gun Violence Through Effective Messaging* was produced a couple of months before Sandy Hook in 2012. One might conclude this was a playbook waiting for a game.

The booklet was so revealing that Peter Jay Gould, executive producer of *Infringed: Second Amendment in the Crosshairs,* called it "80 pages of how to misuse tragedy to mislead people."

"It is terrifying," he said during remarks at the 2013 Gun Rights Policy Conference a couple of months after the guide was uncovered.

Coauthor Workman was first to simultaneously report the existence of *Preventing Gun Violence Through Effective Messaging* in his daily column for *Examiner.com* and the on-line version of *TheGunMag.com*, the latter a monthly print and on-line publication that had replaced the 40-year-old *Gun Week* a year before, and where he serves as senior editor. Within days, conservative bloggers and full-time writers and columnists were writing about this document, many spinning the story with new details that attempted to link it to Democrats, because the people involved in producing the guide worked for firms that had solid ties to the Democratic Party, which has come to be known as "the party of gun control."

Somewhat to the authors' disappointment, very few of those reporters, pundits and bloggers credited the story to its original source. But the important thing was that this information was now "out there" where people could see it.

But what neither of them realized is that *Preventing Gun Violence Through Effective Messaging* was not the only such document that had been prepared to help self-styled "progressives" mount a battle of semantics against the Second Amendment. Also in 2012, a liberal organization called Progressive Majority produced "Voicing Our Values: A message guide for candidates" that was written by the organization's president, Gloria Totten and veteran political consultant Bernie Horn.

While this 70-page booklet covered a wide range of subjects and offered liberal talking points and talking strategies, it was followed up on-line with a 12-page addendum aimed squarely at gun control messaging.

Their multi-section "addendum" to the Message Guide is rather detailed. The sections are headlined:

- Gun Messaging
- How to introduce your argument
- About Background Checks
- About Military-Style Assault Weapons
- About High-Capacity Ammunition Magazines
- How to rebut common pro-gun arguments
- Sources for more detailed talking points

All of this is rather interesting when one reads the "Declaration of Progressive Values" in the initial booklet that contains as its lead item: "First, progressives are resolved to safeguard our individual freedoms. For two centuries, America has been defined by its commitment to freedom.

We must fervently guard our constitutional and human rights, and keep government out of our private lives."

Apparently, that principle applies to everything but the right to keep and bear arms, which is affirmed and protected by what University of Texas law professor Sanford Levinson called "The Embarrassing Second Amendment."

On their website, the Progressive Majority explains what they are all about, and includes this paragraph: "Civil Rights: Every individual's civil rights must be protected; discrimination and harassment based on race, ethnicity, gender, religion, sexual orientation, or physical and developmental ability should be banned."

There is nothing about prohibiting infringement of the right to keep and bear arms. Indeed, their talking points in the "Message Guide addendum" appear to be all about how to push such infringements with clever semantics so as to disguise their intent.

That this document appeared about the same time as *Preventing Gun Violence Through Effective Messaging* should be enough to raise alarms throughout the firearms community. Both the gun control guide and the "Messaging Guide's addendum" amount to road maps showing where anti-gunners want to take the nation, and how they plan to accomplish that task.

Preventing Gun Violence Through Effective Messaging offered advice on everything from using effective rhetoric to dividing National Rifle Association members from NRA leadership. One of the people who prepared the guide was Al Quinlan, a principle of the Washington, D.C.-based firm of Greenberg Quinlan Rosner (GQR), which also has offices in London and Buenos Aires.

According to the guide, Quinlan was part of "a team of communicators" with "decades of experience advising organizations on message development and strategic communications." Other members of this team were Frank O'Brien, creative director and founder of OMP, another Washington, D.C.-based firm, and Jeff Neffinger and Matthew Kohut at KNP Communications, also headquartered in Washington, D.C.

Among GQR's clients had been the Mayors Against Illegal Guns, the Joyce Foundation, several state education associations, Defenders of Wildlife, National Public Radio and the Sierra Club. Among OMP's clients are Planned Parenthood of America and the Natural Resources Defense Council; all liberal organizations that have taken, at various times, positions seen by many in the firearms and hunting communities as supporting gun control or opposing hunting.

A report from the Washington State Public Disclosure Commission filed by the Washington Alliance for Gun Responsibility (WAGR) showed a May 2013 expense of $43,700 paid to GCR for opinion research. WAGR is the organization behind a 15-page gun control initiative filed in 2013 for submission to the 2014 Legislature, and ultimate placement on the November ballot for that year.

According to e-mails obtained from King County by SAF under the public documents law request, WAGR's Zach Silk sent a February 20, 2013 message about progress on gun control measures during that year's legislative session that was copied to Sung Yang, chief of staff for King County Executive Dow Constantine. That e-mail had an attachment headlined "Framing, Message, and Language for Gun Violence Prevention" from GQR. It was a three-page memo to the "Gun Violence Prevention Communications Taskforce" and was essentially a summary of key points in the larger strategy guide.

That was the document that led to Gottlieb's discovery of the 80-page gun control guide.

The playbook's initial revelations roared across the Internet, and other writers began probing deeper, quoting passages from the manual and offering their own links, as the original one was quickly taken down.

The *Preventing Gun Violence* report reminded readers that "most Americans consider the NRA to be a mainstream organization." During its research, GQR asked people which of the following statements came closest to their personal opinion:

• "The NRA is an extreme organization with too much power in Washington that blocks any attempts to reduce gun violence in America."

• "The NRA is a mainstream organization that protects our Second Amendment rights and provides information about gun safety."

The guide addressed Stand Your Ground laws and counseled the use of provocative substitute phrases including "Shoot First" and "Kill at Will," asserting that these terms are "more accurate and persuasive." In reality, those phrases are inflammatory and designed solely to demonize the concept of self-defense with no duty to retreat.

In the process, the guide also identified terms that should be avoided in public debate, among them the phrase "duty to retreat," noting that the requirement may be an established legal principle in some jurisdictions, but it conveys weakness to the public and is "hard to defend."

The gun control playbook is a well-crafted study of semantics and how they may be used to further the anti-gun agenda. Indeed, since the title of the strategy guide actually is *Preventing Gun Violence Through Effective Messaging*, it might be fair to suggest that the title ought to have been "Gun Control Through Effective Messaging."

Emotion Rather Than Fact

"The core frame should be personal and emotional—centered on 'people' and not on facts, laws, or legislation." This was one of the key tips offered in the guide, and gun rights advocates, along with many writers and bloggers who subsequently wrote about the document were quick to stress that this indicated an acknowledgement by gun prohibitionists that they do not have facts on their side so they must appeal to lawmakers and opinion shapers purely on an emotional level.

True enough, as if to emphasize the strategy, the guide noted, "An emotionally-driven conversation about what can be done to prevent incidents…is engaging."

Following a media event in Washington D.C. held just days after the Washington Navy Yard rampage by a man armed with a pump-action shotgun and a week after two anti-gun Colorado state senators were recalled over a gun control vote, ABC News reported that a crowd brought together by Mayors Against Illegal Guns was joined by victims of violent crime.

ABC News' Abbe D. Phillip said "the rally was a show of strength, powered largely by the emotional appeal of survivors." Precisely.

Who can deny the power that a statement from former Congresswoman Gabrielle "Gabby" Giffords, who survived an assassination attempt in Tucson, Arizona can have? Her impaired speech pattern and body movements cannot help but have emotional appeal. When she talks about the need for background checks, people listen. Some notice that she seems to overlook the fact that the man who shot her and killed several other people had gone through a background check when he purchased the pistol he used.

As the gun control playbook advised, "The core frame should be personal and emotional—centered on 'people' and not on facts…"

S. H. Blannelberry writing about the guide for *Guns.com* noted, "But the gun control debate doesn't center around facts. It centers around rhetoric and semantics. It's a war waged with words. And it's the side that does the best job defining and, in some cases, redefining the debate that often has the upper hand."

Calling it "wordplay," Blannelberry observed, "Every gun owner is familiar with how gun-control advocates have used wordplay to their advantage.

"Perhaps the most obvious example is the term 'assault weapon,' which is nothing more than a semiautomatic rifle with a detachable magazine and certain cosmetic features, e.g., pistol grip, flash suppressor, barrel shroud, etc.

"Of course, we know this, but Joe Public may not," he added. "And that's the point. Convince Joe Public that an ordinary and commonly own sporting rifle is an 'assault weapon,' which is to imply that it's an instrument of death and destruction."

The emotion-over-fact strategy can be seen in use frequently when the press covers high-profile shootings, or simply makes them high-profile by the amount of coverage they provide. It has become almost obligatory for reporters to blame "high-powered assault rifles" for every mass shooting, and the deliberately provocative term seems to have become part of the press lexicon. One cannot mention firearm without beefing it up with the descriptive "high powered" term or "easily concealed" if a handgun is the focus.

Blannelberry's wordplay principle can be seen in how the press, and the gun prohibition lobby, itself, continually find new terms that mean the same thing. For example, gun control became gun safety, and more recently it has transformed into gun reform. Organizations that once were happy to describe themselves as Handgun Control, Inc. for example became The Brady Campaign to Prevent Gun Violence.

It becomes a game of verbal sleight-of-hand, and the anti-gun-rights people have become rather adept at it. Whether their tactics came from the pages of the gun control playbook, or provided the foundation for its creation, the long term result is that the 80-page strategy guide is now available to provide a framework upon and around which gun control efforts can be designed, whether big or small.

Of course, following the principle laid down by Chicago Mayor Rahm Emanuel back when he was Senior Advisor to the President for Policy and Strategy for the Clinton administration, these gun prohibitionists – now with a good strategy guide in hand – quickly learned that they "never let a crisis (or a tragedy) go to waste."

Chicago's horrendous murder rate thus becomes not a problem of poor municipal management and a failure of the courts and law enforcement, but the fault of the National Rifle Association and the gun industry. President Barack Obama, who learned early in his career to blame everyone but himself and his ideology for anything that goes wrong, is a skilled practitioner of this game, having learned the ropes in his adopted hometown of Chicago.

When a gang rivalry produced a mass shooting at a Chicago park that left 13 people wounded, including a three-year-old child, Chicago Police Superintendent Garry McCarthy's first reaction was to call for a ban on so-called "assault weapons." That's far easier, and probably safer, than sending his police into high crime areas to round up gang thugs.

The image of a child broadcast on every television station in the Chicago-Indianapolis area, and splashed across the front pages of local newspapers is powerful – emotional – stuff.

Examples Everywhere

While it would be impossible to prove, one can theorize from reading liberal newspapers, watching news broadcasts and listening to the rhetoric of gun prohibition organizations that strategies outlined in the *Preventing Gun Violence Through Effective Messaging* and in the addendum to "Voicing Our Values: A message guide for candidates" are in widespread use, and have been for some time. One might even argue that the gun control guide didn't invent these strategies but merely put them all together. Some of these uses may be inadvertent, but the language of gun control as explained in the playbook has evidently become part of the mainstream press lexicon.

This should concern Second Amendment activists because it signals that they are behind the curve in terms of sending their own message about civil rights, self-defense and self-determination.

For example, a story that appeared in the New Haven, New Hampshire *Register* was headlined, "Gun violence prevention group targets homicides and illegal gun sales."

CT Against Gun Violence (CTAGV) is not an anti-violence organization so much as it is a pro-gun control group. But CTAGV organizers followed a long-standing guideline that was established long before the gun control guide was written that the Left no longer talks about "control" but "violence prevention." It translates to the same thing, but provides just enough cover to the gun grabbers behind such a movement that average citizens only ascertain that this group is opposed to "gun violence."

Well, who isn't opposed to violent crime involving firearms? Most assuredly, organizations that defend Second Amendment rights and represent the interests of millions of law-abiding firearms owners are opposed to violent crime. Indeed, it was the so-called "gun lobby" that produced and championed two of the most effective anti-crime programs of the past three decades, "Three Strikes and You're Out" and "Hard Time for Armed Crime," both the handiwork of staffers from the Citizens Committee for the Right to Keep and Bear Arms (CCRKBA) and its sister organization, the Second Amendment Foundation, essentially brainstorming on their own time and working with various groups to make both projects become reality.

In addition, the National Rifle Association (NRA) was an early supporter of "Project Exile," another program designed to target career armed felons and punish them.

But the CTAGV approach to dealing with "gun violence" does not follow the gun rights groups' efforts. Instead, it appears to follow the strategies outlined in the gun control guide, and so did the newspaper in reporting the group's efforts.

The first paragraphs of the *Register* story seem to follow this strategy:

LaChristopher Pettway, 26, of Bridgeport, was shot on September 9. Pettway's mother, Jacqueline Pettway of Bridgeport, said he was killed while protecting children who were getting off a bus at 2 p.m. that day. She laid her son to rest Sept. 17.

"It is too late for my son, but I have a chance to save another person's life," Pettway said. "My focus now is to get the laws changed so my son's death is not in vain."

In *Preventing Gun Violence Through Effective Messaging* one will find the heading "Overall Messaging Guidance" Rule #1, which says, "Always focus on emotional and value-driven arguments about gun violence, not the political food fight in Washington or wonky statistics."

Rule #2 advises, "Tell stories with images and feelings."

Did the *Register's* story about LaChristopher Pettway not do all of these things in the first couple of paragraphs? A dead young man, killed "while protecting children," his grieving mother determined to make something positive come from her son's death; how much more emotional can one get?

Pettway, also known as "50" and so identified in one account of his demise, was reportedly standing by "the gate" of the Trumbull Gardens housing project in Bridgeport, CT, with 19-year-old Aijaholon "Diggy" Tisdale and a couple of younger teens, according to the *Connecticut Post* in Bridgeport.

A suspect identified as Roderick "Riki" Rogers walked up to them, accused them of having involved in a recent shooting, pulled a .380-caliber pistol and opened fire. Pettway was killed and Tisdale was wounded.

Rule #3 advises, "Don't assume the facts – and don't wait for them."

Right, never let fact get in the way of a good, sensational story. And, always be willing to plant innuendo because tiny seeds have a way of growing into large, believable inaccuracies. As Dr. Timothy Wheeler noted in an opinion piece about the gun control playbook, "After all, who needs facts like police reports or court evidence when you want to harness the power of negative emotions while they're running high?"

Wheeler is the founder of Doctors for Responsible Gun Ownership, a project of the Second Amendment Foundation. He is an articulate and devastatingly effective foil for anti-gun physicians who hide behind their medical credentials to push a political agenda.

Dr. Wheeler's observations about the playbook seem spot-on.

Take, for example, an editorial from the *Bloomberg News* in which lots of support for the policies of anti-gun New York Mayor Michael Bloomberg, who also happens to be the founder of Bloomberg LP, was strongly expressed on the subject of regulating so-called "online gun sales."

The editorial targeted *Armslist.com,* a website "devoted to firearm sales," the piece noted.

"Armslist," the editorial stated, "is precisely the kind of lawless marketplace that the National Rifle Association champions and that the U.S. Senate this year mobilized to protect by scuttling background-check legislation. With the growth of online markets, there's never a need to wait for a gun show; tens of thousands of guns are on sale every hour of every day.

"In an effort to gauge the extent of criminal activity online," the editorial continued, "Mayors Against Illegal Guns analyzed the contact information supplied by prospective buyers in the "want-to-buy" ads posted on Armslist. According to the study, 1 of every 30 gun seekers in the want-to-buy section had a history that would prohibit them from legally possessing a gun.

"Alarming as this snapshot is," said the *Bloomberg* editorial, quoting the report, "it badly understates the true scope of the problem. Only 5 percent of the postings on Armslist are want-to-buy ads: the vast majority of buyers — prohibited and otherwise — respond to 'for-sale' ads, and therefore remain completely anonymous."

The editorial is heavy on semantics designed to alarm, if not inflame, readers. "Lawless marketplace" is a spin on the "Wild West" image of firearms owners that gun prohibitionists have fostered for years. They want average Americans to view gun owners as essentially outlaws who have no moral or ethical foundations and operate beyond the law and common decency.

The *Bloomberg* editorial also planted this, in the first paragraph: "It's not difficult to grasp how a man with a history of gun arrests and mental instability obtained the necessary firepower to commit a massacre at the

Washington Navy Yard earlier this week. Buying a gun, or even an arsenal, is exceptionally easy in the U.S."

What the *Bloomberg* editorial conveniently overlooked is that the Navy Yard gunman, Aaron Alexis, had passed a background check when he bought the Remington Model 870 Express 12-gauge shotgun and a box of 2 ¾-inch 00 buckshot shells two days prior to the attack. Gun prohibitionists endeavor to create the false impression that there are no background checks today, or that someone obtained a firearm without one when they actually passed a background check.

Remember, the suspect in the Aurora, Colorado, movie shooting passed background checks when he bought his guns at retail, as did convicted Seattle Jewish Federation gunman Naveed Haq when he bought two handguns at two different shops in the Tri-Cities area some 250 miles from Seattle. Jared Loughner, the man who opened fire on former Congresswoman Gabrielle "Gabby" Giffords, wounding her and killing several others bought his handgun at retail outlet, and passed a background check.

The list goes on and on to include Sueng Hui Cho, the Virginia Tech killer. Prior to his capture in Utah, even Ted Bundy could have purchased a firearm and passed a background check, because he had no prior criminal history and, besides, he – like other serial killers – did not use a firearm to murder his victims.

But gun control advocates and their media cheerleaders almost invariably overlook this story angle because it would reveal to readers that, despite the shrill intimations that such checks might prevent mass shooters from getting guns, it has not worked out that way.

Misleading Mastery

Award-winning writer Alan Prendergast, writing for *Denver Westword*, noted that the gun control playbook recommends talking points that "seem to rely on shaky or simply inaccurate research."

"One key assertion — that 40 percent of Americans 'have themselves or personally know someone who has been a victim of gun violence' — turns out to be based on proprietary data that can't be checked," he noted. "There's also a claim that all four guns used in the 1999 Columbine High School shootings 'were bought at gun shows without background checks,' which is incorrect. Dylan Klebold's TEC-9 was acquired through an illegal sale, and the seller and middle man did prison time."

Prendergast apparently overlooked the fact that the gun control playbook is crafted for people who conduct their efforts on an emotional level that allows for the throwing around of statistics that are hard to prove and just as difficult to disprove. Nowhere in the guide does it instruct anyone to tell a lie, but by laying out strategies for an emotional battle, that door is certainly opened, albeit inadvertently and presumably unintentionally.

The playbook does encourage activists to use provocative, if not downright inflammatory language to further their arguments. For example, in a section dealing with "Stand-Your-Ground" laws, the guide calls them "shoot first" laws and instructs the user to use that term and "kill at will" because "we should quickly shift to language that positions our argument more persuasively."

Likewise, in the addendum to the Progressive Majority booklet, key talking points are spelled out word-for-word for gun control proponents almost like the script to a play.

For example, on the subject of background checks, the Progressive Majority instructs activists pushing for the more invasive, expanded "universal check" to say this: "The federal background check law has blocked more than 1.5 million illegal gun sales over the past 14 years. The problem is that the law doesn't apply to private sales, so felons can avoid a background check and get any kind of gun, no questions asked…It's time to close the private sales loophole."

The semantics have changed with this, for what once was demonized merely as the "gun show loophole" was now even more encompassing, affecting the kinds of transactions that millions of law-abiding Americans have done for generations: sales or trades of firearms to hunting partners, friends and neighbors, all without the slightest harm to anyone.

Rights advocates were quick to recognize that such expanded checks are designed for one purpose, to lay the groundwork for the next incremental step toward the Utopia where gun prohibitionists believe they are headed, and that step is registration. There is no benign explanation for wanting to establish a registry of firearms and the people who own them. Registration of firearms has only two fundamental purposes: to tax them or to take them.

Americans have become weary of backing down and believe strongly that people have a right, if not a moral duty, to fight back. That fighting spirit has been alive since Lexington and Concord, the Alamo and Pearl Harbor. American heroes don't slink into the shadows, they stand their ground.

It was, after all, Militia Capt. John Parker, who told his company of men at Lexington as British troops entered the village, "Stand your ground. Don't fire unless fired upon, but if they mean to have a war, let it begin here."

Words have meaning, and for the authors and users of *Preventing Gun Violence Through Effective Messaging* and the gun control addendum to Voicing Our Values: A message guide for candidates, the desired effect is not to cast aspersions on an American trait that has been characterized on screen by heroic figures including John Wayne, Clint Eastwood, Charlton Heston and many others, but to associate by reference the act of self-defense with wanton mayhem and murder. Thus, the *Preventing Gun Violence* playbook recommends that anti-self-defense activists "emphasize that these (stand-your-ground) laws escalate everyday conflicts into lethal events."

Has this not been the tactic of concealed carry opponents for decades? Have these public disarmament advocates not repeatedly warned legislature after legislature that passage of "shall issue" concealed carry reforms would result in curbside shoot-outs over fender-bender auto mishaps? Haven't anti-gunners endeavored to create the impression that legally-armed citizens are would-be vigilantes?

Indeed, in the playbook section dealing with Stand-Your-Ground, the third talking point is to "Make it clear that shoot first laws provide cover for gun-toting vigilantes."

As Dr. Wheeler noted in his critique of the playbook, "This is not only a crass attempt to stir bad feeling toward these laws, but perpetuates the lie that they empower victims to become legal aggressors. Stand Your Ground laws simply codify longstanding case law that a person doesn't have to retreat from a violent criminal attack in a place where he has a right to be. He certainly may retreat, but is not required to by law. This is not a new concept, but gun prohibitionists have latched onto it in an attempt to delude the public and weaken gun rights by calling for repeal of Stand Your Ground laws."

Wheeler further notes that "Safire's Political Dictionary describes the ancient rabble-rousing political technique of waving a bloody shirt. He details how the technique was used in ancient Rome and on through the turmoil of pre-civil war America. It is a dubious method based on cynical exploitation of man's less noble nature. It hides facts and reason, and it encourages anger and prejudice. But judging from this gun control playbook, gun grabbing activists and politicians apparently love it."

Dancing in Blood

For many years, firearm civil rights advocates have recognized that following high-profile shooting incidents, gun prohibitionists seem to trip over one another in their rush to the nearest microphone.

Many in the gun rights movement have dubbed this habitual, and predictable, race to exploit a tragedy as "dancing in blood." The term is not meant to be flattering.

In the section dealing with such acts of violence, the playbook notes, under the heading "Don't hesitate to speak out" that "There can be a tendency to adopt a quiet 'wait and see' attitude when a high profile gun violence incident happens. The truth is, the most powerful time to communicate is when concern and emotions are running at their peak. While we always want to be respectful of the situation, a self-imposed period of silence is never necessary."

Spoken like a veteran from a lynch mob.

"In other words," Dr. Wheeler observed, "don't wait for families to grieve or the facts to come out before pointing fingers and pumping up the public's emotions."

That much became horribly evident in the few days following the June 2014 school shooting at Troutdale, Oregon's Reynolds High School. One student was killed, one teacher was wounded and the teenage shooter, who brought a rifle and pistol from home after he got them from secure storage (as authorities described it), took his own life.

Within hours, anti-gun Oregon Congressman Earl Blumenauer, a Portland Democrat representing the state's Third District, sent out a Twitter message that stated, "Another shooting. I always hope tragedy will inspire action. Simple common sense steps make difference. Start w/universal background checks."

Two days after that, Oregon State Sen. Ginny Burdick, described by the Portland Oregonian as "the Legislature's most vocal advocate for stricter gun laws," said the parents of the Reynolds High School shooter "should be held criminally responsible for the death of Emilio Hoffman," the 14-year-old student he shot.

Burdick spared no rhetoric in describing the firearms that the shooter carried, calling them "weapons of war."

As writer S.H. Blannelberry had earlier noted about the gun control guide's authors, "In short, they believe that gun control advocates need to leverage the emotions of the public in the aftermath of a tragedy to push for stricter gun laws, which is exactly what the president attempted to do in the wake of the mass shooting at Sandy Hook Elementary School in Newtown, Connecticut."

The media play no small part in these melodramas, as reporters trying to be first with some new tidbit or sensational with some new angle – all too often demonstrably erroneous – simply cater to, while feeding from, the hysteria generated by gun controllers determined to move their agenda forward.

When *Preventing Gun Violence Through Effective Messaging* was first uncovered, the mainstream press did nothing. Conservative bloggers and pundits have, as shown earlier, written quite a bit about the document.

As we move forward through more legislative sessions and incidents, it will be both enlightening and perhaps darkly entertaining to monitor the activities of the gun prohibition lobby to see which strategies detailed in the playbook are being used at any given moment.

That gun control lobbying organizations and activists will continue following the recommendations contained in the 80-page manual is predictable because, in the final analysis, the emotional argument is essentially all they have. Their penchant for cherry-picking statistics and relying on questionable research suggests that they are running out of gas.

Yet that cannot be taken for granted nearly as much as their ability to rebound with some new horror to once again threaten the rights of millions of law-abiding firearms owners. The end game is what matters, and for gun prohibitionists, eliminating private gun ownership or regulating it so heavily that most gun owners give up is worth a generational effort.

Their strategies, and strategy guide, revealed, it is incumbent upon firearms owners to recognize when an argument is being recycled to fit a new set of circumstances. As the playbook advises on page 57, "If facts don't fit your state, consider an alternative line of argument." Gun grabbers will adapt and change their approach, but always with their traditional agenda in the background.

As the *Preventing Gun Violence* guide notes, "…when talking to broader audiences, we want to make sure we meet them where they are. That means emphasizing emotion over policy prescriptions, keeping our facts and our case simple and direct, and avoiding arguments that leave people thinking they don't know enough about the topic to weigh in."

Translated, this means convincing people to act before they take the time to do a little research so they do "know enough about the topic to weigh in."

It means that gun control advocates should "avoid arguments" that not only challenge them with facts, but leave the audience convinced that they don't know what they are talking about.

Emotion goes only so far in winning a debate. Facts matter, and if gun prohibitionists had facts on their side, they would not need strategy guides that promote "emphasizing emotion" and "avoiding arguments" to achieve their goals.

CHAPTER 2

LIVING IN DENIAL DOES NOT MEAN OWNING A RIVERSIDE HOUSE IN EGYPT

For many years, the gun prohibition lobby has repeatedly argued that more guns in private hands would translate to more murder and mayhem; shootouts at fender benders would become commonplace, more husbands would murder their wives, more cops would die at traffic stops, more children would be slaughtered and America would become a sea of blood.

Actual crime statistics not only did not bear that out, no matter how they might have been spun by gun banners, but actually showed quite the opposite. Violent crime has declined; another reason that the gun control strategy guide stresses emphasizing emotion over relying solely on statistical evidence. Annual release of the FBI Uniform Crime Report, while being admittedly and unnecessarily complicated when it comes to explaining how many people were killed, how they were killed and whether they died as a result of criminal or justifiable homicide, otherwise known as self-defense, showed the decline.

In the aftermath of a massive failure of the Obama administration and Capitol Hill anti-gunners to pass stricter gun control laws in the wake of the Sandy Hook Elementary School attack, the date of May 8, 2013 may stand as a "day of infamy" for anti-gunners because two independent reports, one from the Justice Department's Bureau of Justice Statistics (BJS) and the other from the Pew Research Center, released almost simultaneously, irreversibly put the lie to the "more guns = more crime" myth.

The BJS report said gun-related homicides declined 39 percent from 1993 to 2011, a drop from 18,235 killings to 11,101 over the course of roughly two decades. During that same period, firearms sales across the

United States soared, the number of citizens licensed to carry concealed more than doubled, and contrary to what gun prohibitionists claimed, millions of new gun owners joined the shooting fraternity. All of these factors combined, gun advocates insisted at the time, blew a "Titanic-sized hole" in the entire gun prohibition agenda.

Pew Research reported that the "number of gun homicides per 100,000 fell from 7 percent in 1993 to 3.6 percent in 2010, a drop of 49 percent." Like it or not, that is a staggering revelation for a political movement that had tried to build momentum on the false premise that crime was going up in relation to all the new gun sales that were being recorded, and the equally false promise that applying further restrictions on the right to keep and bear arms by law-abiding citizens would somehow discourage violent criminals.

Indeed, according to figures obtained from the National Shooting Sports Foundation, beginning in the fall of 2006 – perhaps not coincidentally to the takeover of Congress by Democrats, led by Californian Nancy Pelosi as the then-new House Speaker and Harry Reid of Nevada, the new Senate Majority Leader – U.S. citizens began buying more guns.

Background check figures suggest a steady annual rise in the number of transactions, from 8.9 million checks in 2006 to nearly 19.6 million checks in 2012 – more than double – and that suggests people, even those who voted for Democrats, were quickly wary that with the "Party of Gun Control" in power, it would be inevitable that new gun control initiatives would be pushed.

It took the Obama administration a while to get around to it, waiting until after the 2012 elections and capitalizing on the Sandy Hook tragedy to revive and expand a gun control agenda that had been gathering dust for several years as anti-gun liberals waited for the right opportunity. The December 2012 murders of 20 children and six adults by a mentally disturbed young man at the Newtown, Conn., school provided that opportunity.

It did not seem to matter that gunman Adam Lanza, with a history of mental problems and had murdered his own mother prior to his rampage, so there had been no background check or waiting period, nor had there been any licensing process under Connecticut laws because even though the killer was 20 years old and could not legally carry a handgun or get a permit, he didn't bother with the paperwork. He killed his mother, who owned the firearms and had passed a background check to obtain them, and then headed to the school.

None of that mattered to the gun prohibition lobby, because they were quickly out of the gate – anti-gun New York Mayor Michael Bloomberg launched a diatribe even before the bodies had been removed from the Newtown crime scene – with demands for more and tougher gun laws. It also mattered naught that none of the proposed gun law changes could have prevented the Sandy Hook massacre had they been in place.

The most discouraging thing is that gun control proponents know it, but they do not care. They are not out to prevent gun-related crime. Their mission is to prevent gun ownership by penalizing law-abiding gun owners and thus discouraging would-be gun owners from exercising a constitutionally-protected fundamental civil right.

However, gun prohibitionists are not merely reluctant to admit this; they either outright lie about it or quickly shift the subject. They will often launch into diatribes about "gun safety" when the reality is their mantra has little or nothing at all to do with firearms safety.

'Assault Rifle' myth

Another symptom of denial for gun prohibitionists is the controversy over so-called "assault weapons." Proponents of banning semiautomatic look-alikes of military firearms (appropriately called "modern sporting rifles" by the firearms industry for that is what they are, whether used for hunting, predator control, competition or home defense) have tried very hard to ignore another part of the Bureau of Justice Statistics study that the firearms community has long been aware of.

Statistically, about 70 percent of all homicides in a given year, according to available data, are committed with handguns, not rifles. Yet because of rare instances in which semiautomatic rifles have been used, gun banners typified by Senator Dianne Feinstein (D-CA) have zeroed in on them. Indeed, Feinstein's Democrat party has essentially demonized these firearms, according to former District of Columbia prosecutor Jeffrey Scott Shapiro, writing in the *Washington Times*.

"But since the tragic Sandy Hook shootings in Connecticut," he observed, "the Democrats have done everything they can to ban firearms that are in common use. Gun-control advocates have waged a diabolical misinformation campaign, mislabeling AR-15s as 'assault weapons,' a term designed to mislead the public into thinking they're actually machine guns or automatic 'assault rifles,' when, in fact, they only fire one shot at a time, no different than a handgun."

He also had this to say about a move by many states to adopt so-called "nullification laws" that would prohibit enforcement of new federal gun laws that "disregard" both the *Heller* and *McDonald* rulings by the U.S. Supreme

Court: "For once, I'm inclined to side with the states on this matter — at least in spirit, since I know many of the federal laws being proposed by the Democratic Party are unconstitutional."

That is heady stuff from a former prosecuting attorney in the nation's capital, but it reinforces the suspicion shared by many in the firearms community that Sen. Feinstein and her associates are not driven by some altruistic motive for a better world, but to hopefully ban an entire class of firearms and make that socially acceptable, thus setting the stage for another ban somewhere over the horizon.

According to the FBI Uniform Crime Report, in 2012 – the most recent year for which data was available – there were 12,765 homicides of which 8,855 were committed with firearms. Of those, only 322 were known to have been committed with rifles of any kind, and not just semi-auto military lookalikes.

When CBS News anchor Scott Pelley spoke at Quinnipiac University in the Spring of 2013, he admitted that big news agencies were "wrong, over and over again" about major stories they covered, including the Sandy Hook tragedy.

That's a remarkable admission and one that should mean the national news agencies are endeavoring to do something to correct the problem. But they evidently are not where gun control is concerned. If they were, they would take the Bureau of Justice Statistics report and ask some very tough questions of the gun prohibition lobby, including the heads of the Violence Policy Center, Brady Campaign and Committee to Stop Gun Violence.

It was by no small coincidence that late in 2013, Quinnipiac University economist Mark Gius published the results of an interesting study titled "An examination of the effects of concealed weapons laws and assault weapons bans on state-level murder rates" in the journal Applied Economics Letters.

According to the abstract, "Using data for the period 1980 to 2009 and controlling for state and year fixed effects, the results of the present study suggest that states with restrictions on the carrying of concealed weapons had higher gun-related murder rates than other states. It was also found that assault weapons bans did not significantly affect murder rates at the state level. These results suggest that restrictive concealed weapons laws may cause an increase in gun-related murders at the state level."

Had the Gius report been available, Pelley and his colleagues could have easily asked why, if rifles are used in only a fraction of all homicides in any given year, there is a continued push to ban semiautomatic modern sporting rifles? Eliminating such rifles could only reduce homicides by one to three percent and maybe not even that much because there is no evidence that people who kill with a rifle would not just as easily kill with a handgun or shotgun.

With homicides below 13,000 annually, reporters could also ask why the gun control lobby continues to perpetuate the argument that some 30,000 people die each year from "gun violence." It is clear gun prohibitionists are lumping in all suicides, which is an emotional and mental health issue, not a criminal violence issue, and they know it. But it boosts the number of firearms-related deaths that they can attribute to "gun violence" and makes a far more impressive figure when talking to the press.

When utilizing the press, anti-gunners also play fast and loose with the facts. Consider what one gun prohibitionist in the Pacific Northwest wrote when trying to justify a series of measures that would severely erode gun owner privacy and right-to-carry in his region:

"Many people are wondering how a basic, common sense law like universal background checks for gun purchases can fail in both D.C. and Olympia. Polls show that on the state and national level, the idea enjoys the support of approximately 9 out of 10 voters.

"The public acceptance of the idea makes sense," he continued. "After all, we don't get to drive a car if we have a history of drunk driving, so why should somebody with a felony or domestic violence problems or someone involuntarily committed for mental illness be able to buy an unlimited number of firearms at gun shows or online, no questions asked?"

That assertive statement resorts to a familiar tactic: compare gun ownership to driving a car and then make a statement. The author should know that it is already illegal for convicted felons or domestic violence perpetrators to purchase firearms, and likewise for anyone "involuntarily committee for mental illness." He ignores one very important fact reported by the BJS study, which reinforces earlier research done for the Department of Justice.

In 2004, according to the report, "among state prison inmates who possessed a gun at the time of offense, less than 2% bought their firearm at a flea market or gun show." If one were to read further, the study breaks down this figure, showing that 0.8 percent of these criminals actually obtained a firearm at a gun show while 0.6 percent got a gun at a flea market.

The study does not reveal whether the inmate bought the gun at a gun show prior to commission of the crime that put him behind bars; that is, it doesn't say whether he legally bought the firearm before engaging in any criminal act.

Strained reasoning

For a genuine challenge in determining the emotional stability and education level of gun prohibitionists, one merely needs to read comments in on-line Reader Feedback sections of local newspaper websites whenever a gun-related story is published.

For example, one individual argued, "2nd amendmenters (sic) claim they take a 'strict constructionist' approach to the constitution to justify letting almost anyone have any kind of gun they want. Well, they are really following a liberal, 'revisionist' approach in saying the 2nd amendment (sic) covers modern weapons. As a strict constructionist, we must take 'arms' as it would have been understood in the late 18th century - namely muzzloading (sic) rifles and pistols, sabers, and those cutesy cannons you see in Revolutionary War Battlefield parks. So let these people have all the muzzleloaders they want, but keep modern arms unknown to our founding fathers under better regulation! Read the Constitution as it was understood, and no how you wish it meant."

Another anti-gunner insisted, "For the most fearful, anti-social, and violent people in our society, a gun is among their most important possessions. Under better circumstances, these folks would direct their fear and anger randomly. However, the NRA is a powerful organizing force to provide cohesion for their negative energy.

"I am sure you must know a number of elected officials who have worked on gun control issues," he added. "Whenever any of them speak up, they get a rash of violent threats made against them. Of course most of these aren't serious, but you never know when one of them is. To protect your safety and that of your family, it's better to keep your head down and do what they say, live to fight another day.

"Someone recently commented that the NRA is a terrorist organization, and in a certain way, this is true," the statement continued. "Just like al Qaeda, the NRA doesn't often pull the trigger, but instead motivates independent actors to do the dirty work. The NRA Board understood this when it elected its new rabble-rousing leadership."

And these people contend that gun owners are paranoid.

From another publication comes this gem: "More guns purchased for home defense are used for other purposes than home defense. Many of them get stolen when the owner is not home, and then sold to criminals that use them in additional crimes. Or the guns are picked up by innocent or stupid children that shoot themselves, their siblings, or friends. And some of those guns purchased for home defense get used for their convenience in domestic violence.

"We don't know the numbers of the incidents as I describe above," the writer continued, "because the NRA has paid off elected officials to make sure public health studies have never been done."

Naturally, when the gun control lobby gets a favorable vote from a politician it supports with a campaign contribution, that's just "common sense" government at work. But let a politician vote against the newest gun control scheme and that person instantly becomes a paid shill for the evil gun lobby, otherwise known as the NRA.

When anti-gun commentators hit their keyboards, anything can happen. Following the release of both the Bureau of Justice Statistics (BJS) and Pew Research studies on declining gun-related homicides, Media Matters' Timothy Johnson fired up the spin machine, insisting that the nation still needs tighter controls on guns, even if the firearms-related homicide numbers are down. Johnson pontificated that the conservative media is wrong.

"Members of conservative media are trumpeting a government report indicating that gun homicides have fallen as proof that the need for stronger gun laws is unwarranted," Johnson wrote, "while ignoring multiple factors that could account for the decrease. At the same time, firearm violence continues to be a problem as firearm homicides have fallen less than serious violent crime in general and the rate of gun violence in the United States still far outpaces other high-income nations."

In other words, Johnson maintained that because firearm homicides have not declined as fast as other violent crimes, the BJS and Pew data are irrelevant. So, he argued, that proves the need for tougher gun laws still exists.

Johnson resorted to what has become a traditional fall-back anti-gun ploy. He argued that it is simply illogical – in his mind, anyway – that "conservative media" think the crime decline is a significant story, and that it refutes the entire gun control agenda. Liberals habitually consider themselves to be more intelligent than everyone else, so they routinely dismiss dissenting opinions as "illogical" which translates to "irrelevant" in their vocabulary.

"But there is no logic to their arguments that data from the reports constitutes evidence against proposals to strengthen gun laws," Johnson insisted. "Gun availability has been repeatedly linked to higher incidence of firearm homicides, and firearms remain the driving factor of homicides, with 70 percent of murders involving guns. According to an October 2012 report from BJS, the rate of serious violent crime declined 75 percent between

1993 and 2011, meaning that gun homicides are declining at a slower pace than overall crime.

"Other factors may help explain the fall of gun crime since the early 1990s," he continued, "including reductions in lead levels, the end of the crack epidemic, advances in medicine that allow more gunshot victims to survive their wounds, and a declining rate of gun ownership."

He did not explain how reductions in lead levels have anything remotely to do with a decline in the gun-related homicides, nor is there any data supporting the argument that there has been a decline in gun ownership. Data on background checks, firearms sales and the number of guns being sold evidently do not matter since anti-gunners believe, or at least want everyone else to believe, all those guns are being purchased by people who already own firearms.

Essentially, the assertion that gun ownership is declining appears to be the latest urban myth.

"The implicit argument made by conservative media is that there is a causal link between reports of booming gun sales in recent years and the overall decline of gun homicide over the past 20 years," Johnson argued. "But this claim misunderstands how gun ownership has changed during this time period. According to the General Social Survey, household firearm ownership has fallen from 43 percent in the 1990s to 35 percent in the 2000s. Overall household ownership is down from 50 percent in the 1970s. As Daniel Webster, director of the Johns Hopkins Center for Gun Policy and Research, explained to *The New York Times*, 'There are all these claims that gun ownership is going through the roof. But I suspect the increase in gun sales has been limited mostly to current gun owners. The most reputable surveys show a decline over time in the share of households with guns'."

Johnson can "suspect" whatever he wants. According to the National Shooting Sports Foundation, strong gun sales have continued since late 2008, perhaps not coincidentally the year Barack Obama was elected with both houses of Congress still in Democrat control. Like it or not, Democrats are known as "The Party of Gun Control" and they earned that title for entertaining virtually every manner of gun control legislation, from licensing and registration to outright bans.

There is anecdotal evidence to suggest that Johns Hopkins and the General Social Survey were simply wrong. Perhaps researchers have failed or refuse to realize that many gun owners, particularly new gun owners, will not disclose they have firearms in the house. They are under no penalty for being deceptive about gun ownership, and an increasing number of gun owners simply lie when asked the question, perhaps out of privacy concerns or something more troubling. More about that in a moment.

But there is something else. Johns Hopkins and GSS evidently don't pay much attention to Gallup or media reports to the contrary of what might be a pre-ordained conclusion. In October 2011, Gallup noted the following: "Forty-seven percent of American adults currently report that they have a gun in their home or elsewhere on their property. This is up from 41% a year ago and is the highest Gallup has recorded since 1993, albeit marginally above the 44% and 45% highs seen during that period."

Fourteen months later in December 2012, 43 percent of the poll respondents acknowledged having firearms in the home, an indication that different people were contacted and the number shifted. In the 2011 survey, Gallup also noted the following:

"A clear societal change took place regarding gun ownership in the early 1990s, when the percentage of Americans saying there was a gun in their home or on their property dropped from the low to mid-50s into the low to mid-40s and remained at that level for the next 15 years. Whether this reflected a true decline in gun ownership or a cultural shift in Americans' willingness to say they had guns is unclear. However, the new data suggest that attitudes may again be changing. At 47%, reported gun ownership is the highest it has been in nearly two decades - a finding that may be related to Americans' dampened support for gun-control laws."

There was one other interesting point in the Gallup findings. "Republicans (including independents who lean Republican) are more likely than Democrats (including Democratic leaners) to say they have a gun in their household: 55% to 40%. While sizable, this partisan gap is narrower than that seen in recent years, as Democrats' self-reported gun ownership spiked to 40% this year," Gallup said.

Any check with firearms retailers from one corner of the country to the other will quickly reveal that huge numbers of their customers are first-time gun buyers, and these people are very quiet about it with their neighbors, friends and particularly co-workers and supervisors. Perhaps it is to avoid social stigmatism and ostracism promoted by the same liberal media that denies their existence.

Veteran gun owners consider it none of the government's business whether they own firearms, so they definitely are not going to share that information with some survey organization.

The rising national interest in concealed carry also belies the notion that gun ownership is shrinking. Some estimates put the number as high as

11.1 million citizens who have a carry permit or license, and it is statistically impossible for all of those people to be veteran gun owners.

NSSF's Lawrence G. Keane, senior vice president and general counsel, noted in 2012 that civilian possession of firearms in the United States is at an all-time high, while the crime statistics continue to decline. The pattern is continuing even now.

"Women, in particular, seem eager to explore firearms ownership," NSSF said in a bulletin. "Participation by women increased in both target shooting (46.5 percent) and hunting (36.6 percent) in the last decade, according to the National Association of Sporting Goods Wholesalers. Also, 61 percent of firearm retailers responding to an NSSF survey said they saw an increase in female customers in their stores.

"More firearms in civilian possession neither equates to more crime nor to more accidents," the organization noted. "NSSF points out that safe and responsible firearms ownership is the norm, not the exception. With an estimated 85 to 90 million firearms owners in the country, accidental firearms fatalities are at a historic low, a level that industry and other concerned groups are working to maintain through such programs as NSSF's Project ChildSafe, which provides free firearms safety kits to law enforcement agencies nationwide."

Yet with all of this happening, the gun prohibition lobby continues to promote the story line that gun ownership is gradually becoming an anachronism, if not headed for extinction. That seems like so much wishful thinking, and a denial of everything going on around them.

Perhaps the biggest exercise of denial is the inability of gun prohibitionists to understand that it is their very gun control efforts that are driving the gun buying surge. If you tell the American public that it can't have something, or that some commodity will soon be in short supply, people will respond reflexively and go after as much of that commodity as they can get their hands on.

Then comes hypocrisy

For many years, gun control zealots have – with no regard for the difference between a privilege and a constitutionally-protected, fundamental civil right – argued that guns and gun owners should be regulated like drivers and automobiles. Gun owners, according to their logic, should be trained and tested and licensed, and their guns should be registered, which suggests that in their minds, owning a firearm is not a right at all, but should be a heavily-regulated privilege.

See how anti-gunners react by agreeing, and then elaborating that such a regulatory scheme should allow armed citizens to carry guns in any state on their home state license. It would allow guns to be bought and sold across state lines. And nobody goes through a background check to purchase a new or used car, since cars are sold without any kind of check on the buyer's driving record.

This line of reasoning runs counter to the gun prohibition agenda, and while some gun rights activists might consider it treasonous to even enter into such a conversation, it tends to tongue-tie anti-gunners to the point of frustration.

When the National Transportation Safety Board recommended that the blood alcohol limit be reduced to 0.05 for proof of driving under the influence, it ignited a discussion about how people who commit an act of vehicular homicide while drunk are held individually accountable but when someone commits an act of firearm homicide, anti-gunners want to punish the firearm. If the logic of self-appointed "gun safety" advocates were applied to drunks who kill, then cars would be banned, along with quart bottles of whiskey, gallons of wine and cases of beer.

At the time of the proposal, the Associated Press ran a story that recalled "the 25th anniversary of one of the nation's deadliest drunken driving accidents in Carrollton, Ky."

"A drunk driver drove his pickup on the wrong side of a highway, collided with a bus and killed 27 people, 24 of them children," the story said. "The children were part of a church youth group on their way home after spending the day at an amusement park."

This was no less a tragic loss of life than the Sandy Hook school shooting in December 2012. Yet gun prohibitionists would place more emphasis on the Newtown deaths than the bus crash fatalities. Why?

The Associated Press, in reporting the NTSB proposal, noted that drunk driving "claims nearly 10,000 lives a year." That's more deaths than gun-related homicide, which, as noted earlier, numbered 8,855 in 2012, according to the FBI Uniform Crime Report. This is a detail rarely used to bring some perspective to the gun debate.

That same year, according to the Governors Highway Safety Association, about 4,500 people were killed in motorcycle accidents, yet nobody has campaigned to ban motorcycles as a result.

According to data from the Centers for Disease and Control's National Vital Statistics Report, in 2011 – the most recent year for which data was available – there were 38,285 suicides, of which 19,766 were firearm-related.

That leaves 18,519 people who died by other self-inflicted means. Yet it would seem that more emphasis is placed on those firearm-related suicides than on other means.

That same year, 851 people died in firearms accidents, less than 25 percent the number (3,555) who drowned accidentally and about 30 percent (2,621) of those who perished in fires or from smoke inhalation. It's a fraction of the 26,631 people who died in falls.

Combine the number of people who committed suicide with the 11,101 homicides, and the 851 gunshot accident victims, and the total is 31,728. That's still fewer people than those (34,677) who died in motor vehicle accidents, according to the National Vital Statistics Report data, even if you toss in the 222 fatalities listed under the heading of "Discharge of firearms, undetermined intent."

Still, the media attention remains glued to guns, possibly because the gun ban lobby is louder than other lobbies.

Readers will notice that the 2011 homicide figures differ between the FBI Uniform Crime Report and the CDC's Vital Statistics Report by more than 2,500 deaths. The FBI also reported 12,664 homicides that year while the Vital Statistics Report put the number at 15,953.

According to Margaret Warner, Ph.D. at the CDC's National Center for Health Statistics, "The CDC data on firearm homicides are from the National Vital Statistics System (NVSS) Mortality data. The NVSS mortality data are based on information from all resident death certificates filed in the 50 states and the District of Columbia. More than 99% of deaths occurring in this country are believed to be registered. The funeral director obtains demographic data for the death certificate from an informant. For homicides and other non-natural causes of death, a coroner or medical examiner typically is required to investigate and certify the cause of death. Causes of death are processed in accordance with the International Classification of Diseases, Tenth Revision (ICD-10). Firearm homicides can be identified using ICD-10 codes.

"The FBI's UCR Program is a nationwide," Warner continued, "cooperative statistical effort of more than 18,000 city, university and college, county, state, tribal, and federal law enforcement agencies voluntarily reporting data on crimes brought to their attention.

"There are definitional differences in homicides between the two systems," she explained via e-mail to the authors. "In addition, the voluntary nature of UCR may lead to some under ascertainment. For instance, the 2010 number from the UCR/SHR does not include any deaths from Florida and the data from Illinois are "limited" as indicated in the footnote on the table.

"The NVSS has released preliminary data for 2011," she said, "but the final data has not been released. I looked at table 20 of the UCR homicide report showing Murder by State, Types of Weapons, 2011, and note that the total number does not include "murder" in Florida, and that 'limited supplemental homicide data were received' from Illinois."

Warner said this website explains some of the definitional differences between the two systems: http://factcheck.org/2012/12/gun-rhetoric-vs-gun-facts/.

One can determine on his own which data gun prohibitionists will use, depending upon which suits their need at the time they use it. Warner has acknowledged that the FBI data is "nationwide" with lots of input, and that there are "definitional differences...between the two systems."

What does that mean? In the real world, as opposed to a statistical one in which numbers crunchers can sometimes play with data or an emotional one where statistics only matter if they can be spun to support an emotional argument, there can be a "definitional difference." In reality, a murder victim is a murder victim, and dead is dead, but in the Utopian mindset of gun prohibitionists, somehow murder victims who die from gunshot wounds are more dead than those killed with blunt force trauma, knives, boots or bare hands.

CHAPTER 3

THE 'GREAT PRETENDERS' UNMASKED

Perhaps nothing is quite as amusing as watching self-styled champions of gun control reveal their level of ignorance by simply opening their mouths; that is, "avoiding arguments" that might leave people thinking they need to do more research before weighing in.

Such occasions quickly become affirmations of a statement attributed to Samuel Clemens, better known as Mark Twain that put it thusly: "It is better to have people think you a fool, than to open your mouth and remove all doubt."

Piers Morgan, the British anti-gun, former CNN commentator has habitually demonized gun rights advocates on his program. Ultimately his evening program was cancelled, in large part due to his fixation on gun control. When he appeared on *CBS Good Morning* to ostensibly tout his then-new, albeit misnamed, book *Shooting Straight,* he had an embarrassing exchange in which he incorrectly said gun rights are protected by the First Amendment. For a man on a mission to destroy the Second Amendment, he obviously did not know this country's Bill of Rights very well, and he was widely ridiculed for the gaffe.

Coauthor Gottlieb issued a statement about Morgan's flub.

"He should not take himself seriously about guns because nobody else does, either."

Trying to have a rational conversation with Morgan about guns is like filming a recruiting commercial for the gun rights movement. When he signed off at the end of March 2014, he could not resist the temptation to make a few final remarks about gun control in the United States. Perhaps at that point he realized that his disgust with American gun ownership had translated into Americans' disgust with his banal mantra.

Morgan is hardly alone in his shallow knowledge of firearms and related subjects, as seems to be the case with virtually all devoted anti-gun extremists. They don't know about guns except they know they don't like them. This frequently leads to embarrassing foot-in-mouth moments.

Possibly no better example of such political self-humiliation has happened in recent memory than that demonstrated by Colorado Congresswoman Diana DeGette, an anti-gun Denver Democrat who – during the height of that state's controversial push of gun control measures when Congress was also discussing various proposals – appeared at a public forum sponsored by the *Denver Post* and began holding forth on so-called "high capacity magazines" that she wanted banned.

DeGette's name and image were all over the Internet immediately in the wake of remarks she made, revealing what many in the firearms community called a disgusting level of arrogance and ignorance about the ammunition magazines she wanted to eliminate. She was one of Capitol Hill's prime backers of legislation that would ban magazines capable of holding more than ten rounds.

"I will tell you," she said with some animation, "these are ammunition – bullets – so the people who have those now they are going to shoot them, and so if you ban – if you ban them in the future, the number of these high capacity magazines is going to decrease dramatically over time because the bullets will have been shot and there won't be any more available."

DeGette did not realize that magazines can be reloaded and used time and again. Her comments were considered "mind-numbingly stupid" by more than one gun owner and no amount of clarification by her staff could erase the foolishness.

Her gaffe did not stop there. When challenged by a member of the audience who was concerned about the possibility of having to face multiple attackers in his own home, DeGette flippantly told the man, "Good news for you, you live in Denver, the DPD would be there in minutes."

The man responded, "I'll be dead by then."

DeGette replied with a smirk, "You'll probably be dead anyway."

A combination of arrogance and stupidity is never very impressive, particularly when exhibited by someone on an issue that will impact the civil rights of millions.. Members of the audience at that forum were appalled.

DeGette ignored another principle: "When you find yourself in a hole, stop digging." DeGette authored an Op-Ed subsequent to her embarrassing appearance that tried to blame the "gun lobby" for seizing her remarks in attempt to silence and discredit her.

"As I have learned in two decades of work on gun violence prevention issues, the gun lobby takes every opportunity to intimidate, and attempt to silence, anyone who stands up to fight to make our families safer," DeGette wrote at the time. "They have done it for decades, and this week, as I continued my pursuit of common-sense gun violence prevention, I found myself in their sights."

DeGette was quickly assured by various bloggers and gun rights activists that nobody in the firearms community was trying to silence her. Indeed, gun activists were rather energetic about circulating the now-infamous video clip across cyberspace, showing the world how little the congresswoman really knew about the product she was demonizing and attempting to ban. They wanted her comments to be heard and repeated, especially that brief exchange with one of her constituents in which she seemed amused that he might be dead by the time Denver police arrived at his home in response to a violent home invasion.

While DeGette demonstrated an abysmal lack of knowledge about magazines that can be reloaded hundreds of times, as can cartridge clips designed for such guns as the bolt-action Model 1903 Springfield – the "assault weapon" of WWI Doughboys – and the M1 Garand, which was instrumental in America's victory in WWII, the larger question was whether she was an isolated case or a typical anti-gunner. There is considerable evidence to support the latter premise.

For example, Rep. Carolyn Maloney, the New York Democrat who tried to exploit the Boston Marathon terrorist bombing by insisting on MSNBC that passing a new gun law would prevent a repeat of that attack, was seemingly oblivious to the fact that the carnage was caused by a bomb blast rather than gunfire.

"One thing that Congress can do right now is pass the gun safety laws," Maloney told MSNBC. "As it stands right now, the next Tamerlan (Tsarnaev) can go to a gun show and buy all the guns he wants, all the weapons he wants, no problem, no questions asked. I think at the very least Congress should pass sensible gun-safety laws that law enforcement is asking for."

Such a performance reveals how shallow and self-serving the gun prohibition mindset has become.

Can anyone forget Vice President Joe Biden's ludicrous home defense advice to his wife about firing a double-barreled shotgun off the balcony to frighten home invaders, or shooting through a door to discourage them?

As in DeGette's case, the vice president made his comments on video and repeated his advice several times during his effort to push a ban on so-called "assault weapons." He argued that semi-automatic rifles are harder for women, especially, to control than a double-barreled shotgun, a contention that is so demonstrably false as to have been considered ludicrous by anyone other than members of the press and die-hard gun prohibitionists trying to gin up Biden's arguments.

Further damaging Biden's preposterous argument was that fact that in many jurisdictions, discharging a firearm outside one's home in an effort to intimidate or frighten someone is a crime, in some cases a felony.

Joe Biden's reputation for inserting his foot deep in his mouth preceded his election to the office of vice president. Veteran Biden observers should have seen it coming, and many did, dismissing his remarks as "that's just Joe."

The flap began with Biden's interview posted on-line in early 2013 with *Field & Stream*, a popular hunting and fishing journal with a national circulation that has been around for generations. The vice president asserted that experienced big game hunters – which he evidently is not – could argue that, "If you can't get the bear or the deer in four or five shots, you've got a problem."

But Biden was confusing hunting with home and personal protection. Again, on this subject, the vice president ignored Twain's advice and related to the magazine about how he had told a man via the internet, "Well, you know, my shotgun will do better for you than your AR-15, because you want to keep someone away from your house, just fire the shotgun through the door."

Biden recommended a course of action that could lead straight to a legal nightmare for an average citizen and at the very least a nasty home repair bill not covered by insurance. Firing indiscriminately through a door – being unable to see what is on the other side – is a horribly foolish act, the kind of thing that lands people in prison.

In his response to a question about magazine capacity limits, Biden's answer mixed the proverbial apples and oranges:

"If in fact the only thing available was 10 rounds in the AR-15 used by the guy who butchered those children up in Sandy Hook, he would have had to change that magazine three more times. And in that time frame, the police would have been there sooner, saving the lives of one or two or three children who got shot."

Until police can magically "beam" to the scene of a crime as they would in a *Star Trek* episode, their response time will never beat or even tie with the speed of a magazine change.

It was essentially Biden's contention that DeGette parroted at the Denver Post forum just a few weeks later. Her defense of her indefensible remarks and ineffectual magazine capacity limits contended that banning their possession "would give those victims in their sights a fighting chance when the gunman has to stop and reload."

To further try shifting blame from her ignorance to those who challenged and corrected her, DeGette asserted, "In the age of social media, the playbook has taken on a new vicious and viral quality, as half-truths and distorted facts can be spread to thousands of their allies over the Internet for mobilization purposes."

If anyone should know about playbooks, it is the extremist anti-gunner.

In steps the sheriff

What political pretenders repeatedly seem to ignore is the likelihood that their stupidity will be quickly rebutted by a far more credible source of information. In the case of the vice president and the congresswoman, that source turned out to be an Indiana sheriff, appearing in a video produced by the ArmaLite corporation for just such a case.

Enter Sheriff Ken Campbell, who told the authors that the video demonstration debunking misperceptions about magazine capacity was filmed in early February 2013 at the American Institute of Marksmanship. Because of his background as an instructor and rangemaster at the famous Gunsite Academy near Paulden, Arizona, Sheriff Campbell was recruited to provide a no-spin, matter-of-fact explanation of what is in the video. That 14-minute video, incidentally, went viral as soon as it appeared on YouTube.

Sheriff Campbell conducted a series of exercises involving an experienced male shooter and a less-experienced female, as time clocks kept track of their shot strings.

In separate exercises, the male and female shooters fired strings of 30 shots, first using two 15-round magazines, then three 10-round magazines and finally five magazines each loaded with six cartridges. They fired at targets and each of the recorded drills were designed to put hits on these targets to simulate how rapidly a person can change magazines and still hit multiple targets.

The man, identified as "Jim," used a Glock semiautomatic pistol, which is popular with law enforcement and private citizens alike. Jim fired his first string with two 15-round magazines in 20.64 seconds, and then emptied the three ten-round magazines in 18.05 seconds. Finally, using the five six-round magazines, Jim fired his third sequence in 21.45 seconds.

The woman, identified on the video as "Christy," fired the same sequence, with two 15-round magazines in 22.9 seconds, the three ten-rounders in 25.51 seconds and the final five six-round magazines in 26.93 seconds.

Additionally, "Jim" fired 20 rounds from an AR-15 rifle using a single magazine in 12.16 seconds. He then fired 20 more shots using two ten-round magazines in less time, 10.73 seconds. Significantly, "Jim" managed better times with both the handgun and rifle when he changed magazines.

This stunning video effectively put the lie to claims by both Biden and DeGette that someone using limited-capacity magazines will be less a threat to innocent victims, and will thus be delayed in committing a heinous crime, allowing police precious additional time to respond.

The video was obtained immediately by the Citizens Committee for the Right to Keep and Bear Arms and circulated the video across the country.

Perhaps adding some sting to the video presentation, Sheriff Campbell appeared in uniform. While anti-gunners like Vice President Biden will habitually use uniformed officers as a backdrop for some speech about crimes or guns, they will screech at the sight of a uniformed officer or sheriff presenting a pro-gun rights message, or they will ignore it and pretend it doesn't exist…and hope the public has a short attention span.

This became obvious in mid-2013 when 54 of Colorado's county sheriffs joined in a federal lawsuit seeking to overturn that state's newly-passed gun control measures that included a ban on so-called "high capacity" magazines. Likewise, four sheriffs in New York also filed a lawsuit against that state's new anti-gun laws.

It gets the public's attention when law enforcement opposes a gun control law or some anti-gun effort, and the Campbell video was no exception. When he spoke, lots of people listened.

"One of the reasons that the magazine restrictions are being proposed," Sheriff Campbell said, "is the perception that if the active shooter has fewer bullets in magazines he will have to reload sooner and this will create an opportunity for someone to tackle him during the reload."

A demonstration in the video proves how dangerously false that impression can be as both shooters fired rounds from their pistol and then changed magazines in separate sequences. Off to their left, a man is shown in a crouched position. He suddenly rushes toward both shooters from a distance of about 25 feet, at the point they stopped to reload. In neither instance does the man get near enough to disarm either shooter before they are reloaded and can fire again.

CCRKBA focused on that revelation in a press release, "Imposing magazine capacity limits creates a horribly false sense of security. This video puts the lie to this politically-motivated disarmament strategy.

"Magazine capacity limits offer no panacea to the rare mass shootings that have alarmed the country," the group added. "It is time to stop this nonsense and expose magazine limits as the monumental fraud they are."

Misinformation about semiautomatic rifles and pistols by people who want them banned for no other reason than their appearance is easily refuted by facts. However, as far too many public surveys about any number of subjects have shown, too many people allow themselves to remain oblivious to the facts and allow emotion to fuel their decision making process.

How 'bad' ideas become 'good'

One week after the Sandy Hook Elementary attack in Newtown, Connecticut, the National Rifle Association held a press conference to announce its School Shield project, a national program to be headed by former Congressman Asa Hutchinson, which would put armed security in every public school in America.

Depending upon someone's political viewpoint, the idea was accepted as either good, or at least an idea, or ridiculously flawed. It was the latter philosophy that emanated from the White House, where Barack Obama and his administration criticized NRA Executive Vice President Wayne LaPierre for his poor plan and many simply dismissed him as an extremist.

But jump ahead several weeks into 2013, and there is Vice President Biden, in the *Field & Stream* interview, telling the magazine "What we're proposing is 1,000 new school resource officers to show best practices that we help. Just like in the COPS bill, where if a community applies, if a mayor or governor applies for more cops and they meet the need, the federal government will come up with X percent of the cost of that salary for the cop for the next five years. The same way, it would work the same way."

In most places, a "school resources" officer is an armed police officer and everyone knows it. Suddenly, what the NRA had proposed now seemed a good idea, provided that it had the Obama administration's spin attached to it.

Similarly, in Snohomish County, Washington, the sheriff's office there announced in mid-March – about three months after the NRA-crafted school shield project was reviled by the gun prohibition lobby – that it would be placing "school services deputies" in areas where they would be regularly patrolling more than 100 schools in the unincorporated parts of the county.

It was very similar to the NRA proposal with an important twist: The deputies would not be at specific school buildings throughout the school day – as opposed to the NRA's plan of having an armed officer or deputy, or some other specialist – in the building. But, since it was a plan announced by a sheriff's office rather than the NRA, it was accepted by the public as a smart move.

Something quite the opposite occurred in Houston, Texas during the week that the NRA was holding its annual convention there in early May 2013. As reported by local media, a proposal to conduct a gun safety class for elementary school youngsters was announced with quite a bit of fanfare and school administrators thought that was just a grand idea, until they discovered that it was to be the NRA's highly-regarded "Eddie Eagle" class.

Almost immediately, the program was cancelled at a couple of the schools.

For some observers, it was "déjà vu all over again." In 1997, the Washington State Legislature adopted a resolution that allowed the State Superintendent of Public Instruction (SPI) to incorporate the Eddie Eagle program into public schools. But the SPI took no action, and instead of utilizing the gun safety curriculum, it was ignored.

As far back as two decades, the firearms community has been proving that it comes up with solutions that nobody on the anti-gun Left approves of because they are products of, well, the "gun lobby."

Quite possibly the most egregious examples of this sort of hypocrisy came with the famous "Three Strikes" law passed by public initiative in Washington State in 1993. That plan was created by a staffer at a major gun rights organization – the Second Amendment Foundation – and championed by a local radio commentator. The NRA provided some critical funding to push the initiative and it became law.

The idea appealed to lawmakers and voters in other states, and soon there appeared to be something of a social tsunami at work across the landscape. People decided that it was time to lock up violent repeat offenders and keep them off the streets.

The political Left thought it a disgusting idea invented by the "gun lobby" to divert attention away from the need to restrict gun rights until then-President Bill Clinton hailed prison sentences given to some repeat offenders, and then suddenly it wasn't so bad an idea after all. According to an account on Wikipedia, after California adopted a similar measure in 1994, murder statistics began declining. In Los Angeles, the homicide numbers dropped by more than two-thirds from 1992 to 2010, as reported by NPR.

Naturally, anti-gunners found any number of reasons that these homicide statistics had declined, and none of them gave credit to the effect of "Three Strikes" laws. The same occurred following passage of "Hard Time for Armed Crime" in Washington State.

Apparently, for the anti-gun lobby, what separates good ideas from bad is whether they have the initials "NRA" attached to them. This pattern has been so often repeated that it has become almost part of the political process, and it underscores how the gun prohibition movement has become the haven of hypocrites.

Gun prohibitionists cannot seem to grasp the concept of punishing criminals and leaving law-abiding citizens alone.

One possible exception to this long-standing pattern came in the fall of 2012 when the Citizens Committee for the Right to Keep and Bear Arms was first to support a proposed crackdown on armed juvenile thugs via legislation proposed by the King County Prosecutor's office in Washington State. The same proposal also got the nod from Washington Ceasefire, the Pacific Northwest's most vocal anti-gun organization.

The legislation did not survive its first go-around with the state legislature the following January, but CCRKBA's approach surprised local reporters.

The 'needs' test

It has become particularly revealing about the mindset of gun prohibitionists who have tried to marginalize the Second Amendment as nothing more than a highly-regulated privilege carefully managed by the government, when they invented the "needs" standard as a means of belittling the right to keep and bear arms.

This raises a question about the anti-gun movement's fealty to the Constitution because if they have so little grasp of what that document is about regarding one amendment, it is no stretch of credulity to presume they have as little regard for other civil liberties.

California Sen. Dianne Feinstein, a vehemently anti-gun product of San Francisco who tried unsuccessfully to impose a gun ban in the Bay City back when she was mayor, is one of those who believes in the "needs" test.

During debate on her ill-fated attempt to once again ban semiautomatic rifles and pistols through legislation, Sen. Feinstein crossed verbal swords with Texas Sen. Ted Cruz. Insisting that her bill would exempt some 2,200 firearms, she argued, "Isn't that enough for the people of the United States? Do they need a bazooka? Do they need other high-powered weapons that other people use in close combat? I don't think so. So I come from a different place than you do."

Sen. Feinstein and her contemporaries in the anti-gun movement can think whatever they please, but they cannot reinvent the first ten amendments to the Constitution as a "Bill of Needs." Whether she thinks someone "needs" a particular firearm is of little consequence to what is protected as a civil right, except perhaps in her own mind.

And note that she employed one of the favorite diversionary talking points of the anti-gun movement, the "bazooka" (or tank, artillery, mortar; some type of heavy military weapon) example, as in "You don't need a bazooka to hunt deer!" It is, of course, a red herring that has nothing at all to do with the actual discussion, but is only inserted in an effort to portray the arguments of gun owners and advocates as ridiculous and extremist.

In that same context, the "needs" argument has been offered time and again by gun prohibitionists who would have us believe that it is acceptable to ban certain firearms or a whole class of firearms, simply on the pretext that "you don't need" such a firearm to "hunt ducks (or deer.)" By offering that argument, they would further have the public believe that the Second Amendment was all about hunting, which it is not.

True, it was one of the reasons offered by Justice Antonin Scalia in his 2008 Supreme Court majority opinion in the case of *District of Columbia* v. *Dick Anthony Heller* for the existence of the Second Amendment, but only perhaps as an adjunct. When the Second Amendment was written, it was common to hunt with a firearm to put food on the table. But the authors had also just concluded a war of rebellion against the English government, and they wanted to assure that they would have the means to protect themselves, and their nation, from tyranny foreign or domestic.

Justice Scalia's historical research on the Second Amendment was extensive and devastating to long-standing arguments by gun prohibitionists about what the right was all about. Fat Left anti-gunners, of course, continue to this day to reject the *Heller* ruling as a "rewrite of history" by an extremist right wing activist high court.

Thus, the invention of the "needs" standard became a fall back strategy in the effort to minimize the right to keep and bear arms to the level of a "need" to keep and bear arms. Today their argument is that there is no "need" for a so-called "assault weapon" to hunt game birds and animals. Tomorrow, it might become a "need" to use a rifle with a telescopic sight.

Likewise, the "needs" standard is applied to ammunition magazines. Countering the argument about magazine capacity is rather simple.

When the assertion arises that magazines with capacities greater than ten cartridges are needed "only for killing large numbers of people," one can quickly leave ant-gunners stammering by asking, "Then why do police need them? Are you suggesting that the police may consider killing large numbers of citizens? For what reason?"

It is very much like challenging anti-gunners who simply contend that only the police should have guns. Typically, the same people who hold that opinion really do not like police that much, so this challenge occasionally gives them pause, or they quickly try to change the subject.

A variation of the sham "needs" argument that has become popular with the Left, meaning that it is over-used, is that the notion of citizen resistance to a tyrannical government in the 21st Century would be tantamount to public insanity because of the powerful military.

As J.D. Tuccille observed in *Reason Magazine*, "At this point, many self-defense activists respond that the need for guns has to do with the ability to defend against tyrannical government. Then gun controllers chirp, 'but you can't defeat tanks and nuclear weapons with rifles!' thereby demonstrating that they don't keep up with the war in Afghanistan and skipped their history lessons about some difficulties the U.S. military ran into in a place called Vietnam."

Tuccille demolishes this particular anti-gun argument with his brief observation, but gun prohibitionists are a persistent bunch, and being made the fool has yet to discourage them for very long. The "needs" argument does gain traction with far too many people, so it has become something of a staple in the gun control playbook. That doesn't make it right, but it does make it effective.

'I support the Second Amendment'

When he appeared on CBS's *Face the Nation* following the Sandy Hook massacre in mid-December 2012, perennially anti-gun Sen. Charles Schumer (D-NY) insisted that the political left needs to "admit there is a Second Amendment."

From a man with Schumer's background of trying everything possible to erode the right to keep and bear arms dating back to his time in the House of Representatives, the New York liberal raised some eyebrows with the remark.

Schumer is one of the great pretenders who insist at every opportunity that they "support the Second Amendment," while their actions belie the statement. At least in Schumer's case, he didn't waste much time trying to perpetuate a myth. Moments later, he insisted that Congress needed to "ban assault weapons...try to reinstate the assault weapons ban" and limit the capacity of ammunition magazines.

According to a recount of his appearance on the *Huffington Post*, Schumer also reminded the CBS hosts and their viewing audience that, "once we establish that there is a constitutional right to bear arms we should have the right admit, and maybe they'll be more willing to admit, that no amendment is absolute after all."

The senior senator from New York is something of a text book example of forked tongue lip service toward the right to keep and bear arms. While begrudgingly admitting that the right exists, he quickly demands that conservatives agree that it is open to erosion.

For Schumer and gun prohibitionists like him, the pretense of Second Amendment support is transparently thin, and it vanishes entirely the moment an opportunity presents itself to vote on some issue that ratchets down on gun rights.

Schumer and other Capitol Hill anti-gunners are cognizant of the fact that when the issue of gun rights has been placed on the ballot, people do not vote away their rights. That's why gun control has historically been created by legislation rather than referendum or initiative. It is also why websites that monitor how politicians vote on important issues have become so popular.

The very notion that one "supports" a civil right is ludicrous because citizens do not "support" rights; they exercise them and live by them. People can support charitable causes or sports teams, but when it comes to a civil right, you either live by it or you don't.

When former and perhaps future presidential candidate and now former Secretary of State Hillary Clinton was campaigning in 2007 for the Democrat nomination to run as president the following year, she was caught by the *Des Moines Register* in one of these "gotcha" moments regarding her "kinda-sorta" belief in the right to keep and bear arms. Immediately after professing her support for the Second Amendment, she commented, "But I also believe in smart laws that keep guns out of the hands of criminals and terrorists."

This sort of disingenuous doublespeak has separated many a candidate from ascension to public office, and it was certainly part of Clinton's downfall. It has become almost routine for a candidate to say, "I support the Second Amendment, *but...*"

What is annoying about this is that they honestly think all of the people buy that simply because some will sucker for what sounds like a "reasonable" caveat; i.e. invasive background checks, ratcheting down on gun shows, bans on so-called "assault weapons" and on down the laundry list of anti-gun talking points until the Second Amendment they support is not a right at all, but a heavily-regulated privilege.

The greatest pretense

Perhaps the greatest pretense of the Great Pretenders is that they are "progressive" and enlightened, placing them somehow above the fray and certainly ahead of the average American gun owners, whom they often characterized as bigots and rednecks.

All-too-frequently, the discussion becomes emotional, and it can quickly go overboard. It happens a lot in print when people passionate about an issue hit the keyboard.

When it comes to encouraging visceral social prejudice nobody does it better than a gun prohibitionist, especially one employed as a journalism professional.

Following the ricin scare in Spring 2013, Becky Sarwate, writing on the *Politicus USA* website, attempted to blame the NRA and Executive Vice President Wayne LaPierre directly for the attacks directed at New York Mayor Michael Bloomberg and President Barack Obama, among others.

"Real-life villains exist within the ranks of overreaching lobby groups," Sarwate wrote, "inciting chaos under the guise of Second Amendment defense.

"I'm no prosecuting attorney," she added later, "but it seems to me that there's a direct correlation between the prolific, fear-inciting rhetoric of Wayne LaPierre and the NRA, and the homicidal threats against the lives of pro-gun control elected leaders. Is a bystander who knowingly allows harm to occur guilty of something? If the answer is yes (and it is), then Wayne LaPierre is an accessory to each and every one of these ricin crimes. He may not have supplied the chemicals, but he and his group continue to dish out motive in dangerous, irresponsible bucketfuls.

"Haul him to the precinct," she demanded, "turn on the hot lights and file some charges. I'm serious. If it's illegal to yell 'Fire!' in a public place and incite a riot, there should be no distinction between trumping up an imagined threat to the Second Amendment and standing smugly aside as violence ensues."

And then there was the opinion piece by Marshall University journalism professor Christopher Swindell that appeared in the Charleston, WV *Gazette* that left many wondering how he could be allowed to teach journalism.

"The NRA advocates armed rebellion against the duly elected government of the United States of America," he asserted. "That's treason, and it's worthy of the firing squad. The B.S. needs a serious gut check. We are not a tin pot banana republic where machine gun toting rebel groups storm the palace and depose the dictator.

"Normally, I am a peaceable man," he continued, "but in this case, I am willing to answer the call to defend the country. From them.

"To turn the song lyric they so love to quote back on them, 'We'll put a boot in your ---, it's the American way'," Swindell wrote.

"Except it won't be a boot," he snarled. "It'll be an M1A Abrams tank, supported by an F22 Raptor squadron with Hellfire missiles. Try treason on for size. See how that suits. And their assault arsenal and RPGs won't do them any good."

He concluded, "And when the next domestic terrorist with an assault rifle comes along, we can blame the leaders and fringe of the NRA for arming them."

Swindell could have made room in his classroom for Donald Kaul, the "cantankerous liberal columnist" – as described by News Busters, anyway – who came out of retirement to launch his own invectives toward the NRA.

His suggestion was to "Declare the NRA a terrorist organization and make membership illegal. Hey! We did it to the Communist Party, and the NRA has led to the deaths of more of us than American Commies ever did. (I would also raze the organization's headquarters, clear the rubble and salt the earth, but that's optional.) Make ownership of unlicensed assault rifles a felony. If some people refused to give up their guns, that 'prying the guns from their cold, dead hands' thing works for me."

This came after also suggesting that "owning a gun should be a privilege not a right."

It was Kaul who wrapped up his diatribe with the now-infamous observation that after repealing the Second Amendment and declaring all NRA members terrorists, he would "tie Mitch McConnell and John Boehner, our esteemed Republican leaders, to the back of a Chevy pickup truck and drag them around a parking lot until they saw the light on gun control."

The greatest pretense of all is that professional journalists with these attitudes can never do what a journalist is supposed to do: Look at both sides of an issue in an objective manner and present those sides to the viewers or readers and allow them to reach their own conclusions.

One might just wonder who is the real promoter of violence, the NRA – which teaches firearms responsibility to millions of Americans – or the journalists who advocate killing NRA members because they choose to exercise a civil right?

CHAPTER 4

DIVERSITY IS GREAT, SO LONG AS IT CONFORMS TO THE ANTI-GUN AGENDA

When the Citizens Committee for the Right to Keep and Bear Arms and its sister organization, the Second Amendment Foundation, launched a video advertisement suggesting that the "real war on women" – a not-so-subtle reference to the one that was invented by Democrats during the 2012 campaign cycle that demonized Republicans – was about choice…to own a firearm, it raised hackles on the anti-gun Left.

This war, according to SAF, which publishes *Women & Guns* magazine, and CCRKBA, is the very real campaign to discourage women from owning firearms for personal protection. According to anecdotal evidence from several sources, the campaign is failing, because a growing number of women have not only been buying guns, they are getting training and licenses to carry.

The SAF/CCRKBA effort struck a raw nerve with liberals, who were not happy that one of their strategic hot button slogans had been turned back on one of their pet political core beliefs – gun control – and that it was effective. So effective was the message, in fact, that Laura Beck, writing on the *Jezebel* website, furiously declared the message to be "hilarious garbage" in the apparent hope that she could marginalize its content, and make it irrelevant. In the process, she simply directed more public attention to the 30-second spot, defeating her own purpose.

When liberal anti-gunners have no direct defense of a position, they try to shift the subject, which Beck did by asserting that armed personal protection should be a non-issue because violent crime has declined. She also criticized the advertisement because it suggested that a gun might be kept in the house for personal protection against someone bent on committing a crime. The message depicted a grandmother huddling with her grandchildren in a closet after one of the youngsters spots a thug trying to enter the house. In the closet, the grandmother calls the police while someone tries to turn a doorknob, and a message then flashes on screen that the average response time for police to a call is 11 minutes.

For those who want everyone to depend upon the police to rescue them, and not take responsibility for their own safety, this is a subject they avoid. But it is the reason that the adage "When seconds count, police are minutes away" has become iconic within the firearms community.

Beck attempted to change the focus, contending that guns in the home kill more children than cancer, which did not address the issue of personal protection against a crime in progress. She used as a reference a story in *USA Today*, that relied on material from the anti-gun Brady Campaign Against Gun Violence. This information referred primarily to firearm-related injuries to children, not fatalities. *USA Today* spun its story by noting "guns still kill twice as many children and young people than cancer, five times as many as heart disease and 15 times more than infection, according to the *New England Journal of Medicine*."

So, instead of just killing "children," the story now included "young people" as part of the equation.

This is typical of how anti-gunners play games with statistics to make things look more serious or urgent than they really are. As the playbook advises, "Use statistics to reinforce an emotional argument, not to replace it."

For example, take this passage from a *USA Today* story about children and firearms accidents: "Nearly 800 children under 14 were killed in gun accidents from 1999 to 2010, according to the Centers for Disease Control and Prevention. Nearly one in five injury-related deaths in children and adolescents involve firearms."

Break out the pocket calculator and do some basic division. Over the course of an 11-year period, "nearly" 800 children under age 14 died in firearms accidents. That averages fewer than 75 children and young teens for each year in a nation of 250-300 million citizens who own in excess of 200 million firearms according to some estimates. While the accidental death of any child is a tragedy, regardless the cause, far more youngsters drown each year or die in car crashes, as we established earlier

But for the rabidly anti-gun Left, it is considered bad form, even hostile, to not take the original figure as a sign of an epidemic. It is worse to compare data and show that the way the information is presented amounts to nothing more than spreading hysteria.

According to data from the National Center for Health Statistics, National Vital Statistics System in 2010, "unintentional firearm" deaths did not rank among the top ten causes of death in either the 1-4 or 5-9 age groups, and only accounted for 26 fatalities in the 10-14 age group.

Meanwhile, 436 tots in the 1-4 age group drowned, 134 more drowned in the 5-9 age group and 117 died from drowning in the 10-14 age group.

According to the Centers for Disease and Control's report headlined *Unintentional Drowning: Get the Facts*, "From 2005-2009, there were an average of 3,533 fatal unintentional drownings (non-boating related) annually in the United States — about ten deaths per day. An additional 347 people died each year from drowning in boating-related incidents.

"About one in five people who die from drowning are children 14 and younger," the report added. "For every child who dies from drowning, another five receive emergency department care for nonfatal submersion injuries." When gun owners offer these statistics to gun prohibitionists, suddenly the data, and the argument, become "irrelevant." They simply do not care to hear it, and they quickly attempt to dismiss it, especially when they're in a debate situation.

But the ploy does not always work. In one devastating appearance before Colorado lawmakers in early 2013 who were debating that state's extremist gun control proposals including a ban on campus carry, rape victim Amanda Collins delivered a blistering rebuttal to Democratic State Sen. Evie Hudak's sneering dismissal of her argument that if she had been armed the night of her attack, the rapist would have been stopped. That man later attacked and murdered another woman.

Hudak, however, engaged in what Second Amendment scholar David Kopel called an outrageous display of "self-righteous, ignorant bigotry."

Speaking to Collins in front of a crowded room, Hudak told the rape victim, "I just want to say that, actually statistics are not on your side even if you had a gun. And, chances are that if you would have had a gun, then he would have been able to get that from you and possibly use it against you.

"The Colorado Coalition Against Gun Violence says that for every one woman who used a handgun to kill someone in self-defense, 83 were murdered by them," the senator added for good measure.

Collins tactfully responded, "Respectfully, senator, you weren't there."

Hudak reportedly later apologized to Collins for her insensitivity, but only after she saw that public reaction to her remarks was politically toxic.

Collins, however, became something of a sensation in the pages of a National Rifle Association magazine, she had the chance to tell her story. The NRA article prefaced her remarks by pointing to Sen. Hudak's comments, describing the exchange as, "the Democrats' war on women was unleashed."

Collins, who had been attacked in October 2007 at the University of Nevada at Reno, explained that she had martial arts training and a concealed carry permit. However, campus policy forbade the carrying of her handgun, and she was overpowered by her attacker.

Said Collins in her NRA "First Person" article, "I'm infuriated with the lawmakers and administrators who rendered me defenseless that night, but I'm even more frustrated with the passivity of other women, especially women legislators. So many of them criticize others for trying to impose personal views about a woman's 'right to choose.' Where were they to defend my choice? …

Essentially, I was legislated into being a victim," Collins said.

She also observed that it is mortifying to hear "lawmakers with an agenda" suggesting that women should just carry whistles. Insisting that she will "never again be defenseless" against an attacker, she professed that she is "adamant that no one—whether the vice president or a state legislator—will violate my dignity a second time by trampling my right to defend myself no matter where I am."

Think Pink.

Beck's sneering outrage at the CCRKBA/SAF video and her attempts to vilify its message because it ran counter to the liberal/"progressive" agenda was no less hostile than what occurred in Seattle, Washington, also in the spring of 2013 when some unidentified and enterprising individual put up posters promoting gun ownership by gays throughout the city's Capitol Hill area and also in Olympia, the state capitol.

Hell hath no fury like a liberal confronted with reality, considering remarks that appeared in Think Progress and the on-line commentary at *The Stranger* – the latter a popular Seattle alternative newspaper – to the pro-gun posters.

One poster showed two females, one of whom is armed with an AR-15 rifle, and it carried this message: "Some people dislike gays. Others dislike guns. We should not base our laws on personal dislikes." The other had a cartoon of two males holding guns and it included this statement: "We won our right to marry…now it's time to defend our right."

Liberals were infuriated because the poster messages asked questions and made statements obviously aimed at providing gay citizens a different perspective on gun ownership. That is considered verboten by the anti-gun establishment; targeting a group that traditionally has been owned by liberals and Democrats. To the liberal elite, that is tantamount to poaching or livestock rustling.

Both posters had a QR code that took people to a website apparently created by Oleg Volk, proprietor of the popular Gun Rights Media (GRM).

The first website asked visually whether a gun is a "useful tool" or "liability." If clicking "liability," one arrived at a questionnaire that challenged traditional liberal anti-gun dogma. Clicking on the "useful tool" image took users to several other links, including GRM.

At *The Stranger*, writer Cienna Madrid criticized the questionnaire reached by clicking "liability."

"The questionnaire is supposed to underscore how important it is for you to be armed to the teeth all times," Madrid wrote. "The arguments aren't new or particularly convincing, I just find it striking that a traditionally conservative movement is branching out to recruit gays and lesbians."

It might have been educational to ask Madrid what was wrong with outreach to gays and lesbians. They have the same self-defense and Second Amendment rights as any other citizen. After all, the Pink Pistols is a national organization created by gays to promote firearms ownership and provide support for gays and lesbians who make that choice.

But the reaction in Think Progress and *The Stranger* suggested that trying to educate the gay community about firearms, personal responsibility, voting and self-defense is tantamount to heresy.

The image of legally-armed gays and lesbians being ready and able to defend themselves simply does not correlate with the Left's caricature of gun owners as low-brow, knuckle-dragging militia extremists.

Madrid and others like her should be challenged to explain just what it is about such posters that offend them more. Was it the firearms educational effort or the possibility that it just might erode what they consider a core voting bloc – which they take for granted at every election cycle – and influence some in the gay community to vote for gun rights? That is a valid question, and one that gun prohibitionists find it difficult to answer candidly, so they almost invariably try to change the subject or to simply characterize the gun community as collectively homophobic, declare victory and go home.

The controversy became so heated that the Pink Pistols, which is based in Philadelphia, issued a statement that it was not responsible for the pro-gun posters. "These posters were not created, or distributed around Seattle by the Pink Pistols.

"The Pink Pistols believes in the lawful self-defense of the GLBT (gay-lesbian-bisexual-transgender) community," the group said in a press release. "Where it is lawful, we believe in the use of concealed firearms for this purpose, because those are statistically the best tools for the job. They are only properly used to defend against imminent death or grievous bodily harm."

However, the organization took issue with the poster that depicted the two men with guns and the message "We won our right to marry…and now it's time to defend our right" because it had a provocative sub-text that said, "And we sure as hell aren't going to take s--- from homophobes in the process."

Reacting to that poster, the Pink Pistols said the message "would not qualify for self-defense using deadly force, unless it was in response to an attack that threatened death or serious bodily harm. This poster does not adequately address the core values of the Pink Pistols mission statement."

"We believe that all persons, gay or straight, should have all of their rights all of the time," the Pink Pistols press release stated. "We believe that a person's civil rights are worth defending. We believe that legislation should be the result of rational deliberation, with the purpose of addressing issues, instead of demagoguery, with the purpose of appeasing voters."

"Those who are offended by these posters, we cannot help you," the Pink Pistols said. "We did not post them. Perhaps it was an individual, or another GLBT firearm organization."

Regardless who was responsible, the enterprise got the attention it was seeking. It offended people on more than one level, but in the final analysis to Liberals the ultimate offense was that the posters appealed to the oldest human right, that of self-preservation/self-defense.

Politically correct profiling

Profiling on the basis of race, gender or religious background is universally condemned in the U.S. Profiling gun owners, however, gets the nod from the politically correct "progressive" Far Left because pigeon-holing gun owners as any of the following stereotypes are perfectly acceptable:

Racists

Sexists

Homophobes

Child Molesters

Anti-government extremists

Wife beaters

Neanderthals

Morons

Profiling became something of an issue in 2013 when a federal judge ruled that Joe Arpaio, the famous sheriff of Arizona's Maricopa County, had allowed his agency to engage in profiling.

There is a biting adage floating around cyberspace that puts the profiling hypocrisy in perspective: "We are told not to judge all Muslims by the actions of a few crazies, but we are told to judge all gun owners by the actions of a few crazies."

Indeed, that has happened, but when confronted with this brutal reality, about the best one can hope for is "Well, that's different." How it is different is never adequately explained. But the childish excuse seems to suffice for anti-gunners, who refuse to understand why someone would want more elaboration.

One only needs to look at recent history.

When Adam Lanza, who was obviously mentally disturbed, opened fire at Sandy Hook Elementary in Newtown, Conn., in mid-December 2012, killing 26 people, he became a poster child for gun control. Gun prohibitionists pushed to ban a whole class of firearms – so-called "assault weapons" because Lanza used one that had been purchased by his mother legally. Just before launching his killing spree at the school, Lanza killed his mother at her home not far from the school.

This tragedy occurred about five months after the infamous "Batman Massacre" at a theater in Aurora, Colo. That event shook Colorado because the alleged gunman, who was taken into custody shortly after the shooting, apparently had scouted theaters in advance. The one he picked was visibly marked as a "gun-free zone" where law-abiding citizens could not carry concealed even if they were licensed to do so.

The alleged gunman, James Holmes, apparently planned the attack in detail. He evidently did not believe he would be returning to his apartment because when authorities went there to search for evidence, they discovered the place had been elaborately booby-trapped with explosive devices to create even more carnage.

These madmen do not represent the tens of millions of law-abiding gun owners, including those who own semiautomatic modern sporting rifles for any number of reasons including hunting, home defense, predator control, competition and recreational target shooting. Yet in the wake of their attacks, the gun prohibition lobby immediately launched a massive effort to force new laws with onerous restrictions onto every firearm owner.

Some anti-gunners wanted to register those rifles already in private hands, and ultimately build a database of all of the owners. As mentioned earlier, this sort of rhetoric raises alarms among gun rights activists who consider registration took be the precursor of confiscation.

These two incidents allowed gun prohibitionists to demonize every citizen who owns an AR-15 type rifle and standard capacity magazine. By extension, anti-gunners demonize all gun owners, including the millions of citizens who have concealed carry licenses and permits, who have repeatedly been shown to be the least likely of all citizens to misuse firearms.

Yet in all of the debate about the merits of new gun measures, or lack thereof, even many in the gun control community were willing to acknowledge that they would not be a panacea to violent multi-victim attacks. Despite these admissions, anti-gunners in Colorado were able to push through a plethora of gun control measures. These new laws led eventually to two recall efforts aimed at politicians who supported the restrictions. Additionally Colorado suffered the loss of million of dollars in revenue because some businesses moved their operations out of the state. Equally devastating was the fact that many hunters and gun owners boycotted Colorado, refusing to spend their tourism dollars there.

Perhaps Colorado's greatest loss was with Magpul Industries, the maker of large-capacity ammunition magazines used with AR-15 rifles and other semi-autos. Colorado guides and outfitters, sporting goods stores, motels and restaurants also took a financial hit.

It did not appear that the gun prohibition lobby in Denver took any notice of the financial impact. Once again, ideologues demonstrated that their agenda was more important than the jobs and revenue lost to the Colorado citizens and state treasury.

They had "done something" to make the state's gun owners somehow accountable for the mass shooting in Aurora, and another one that hadn't even happened in their state. How any of this could have prevented these attacks was not adequately explained, but for the devote anti-gunner, the mere fact that he or she had been instrumental in passing a new gun law – regardless its ultimate effectiveness as a crime prevention measure – was a trophy.

Trophy legislation is a big deal with gun prohibitionists. The ten year ban on so-called "semi-automatic assault weapons" was a trophy statute that was so ineffective in actually reducing criminal violence that Congress allowed it to sunset in 2004. A study commissioned by the Clinton administration came to the conclusion that the ban had not provided a significant result.

Still, anti-gunners cling to the ban and insist that it was working because crimes committed with the banned firearms declined. What they're not acknowledging, however, is that crimes were still committed with guns that weren't banned, and primarily with handguns, which are the more commonly-used in crimes. Rifles are used in a fraction of all gun-related homicides, and the yearly FBI crime data confirms this. The same goes for shotguns, and gun prohibitionists know it because they are aware of this data.

The Left's dilemma with women

There is, perhaps, no greater credibility dilemma for the liberal anti-gun Left than its invariably hypocritical attitude about women and guns. As noted previously a video message reminding women that they can be responsible for their own safety, and the safety of their families, by arming themselves was greeted like toxic waste by the gun prohibition lobby, if they didn't try desperately to ignore it and get everyone else to ignore it, too.

For more than a generation, the Left has pushed the idea of women in combat, and women as police officers, sheriffs' deputies, armed park rangers and transit police, and even Texas Rangers. As all of those things came to pass people overlooked the fact that all of these women demonstrated that they can use firearms responsibly and lethally in armed confrontations.

While this may seem just fine with the Left because it shows "empowered" women who can very capably take care of themselves and others, that notion seems to disappear almost immediately when female private citizens entertain the thought of keeping a gun handy for personal protection. For some unexplained reason, the thought of an armed woman is distressing.

This was perhaps best explained by writer Mike Sweeney of Massachusetts, writing for the *Daily Caller*. He wrapped his remarks around an incident that happened in Oregon that became an outrage in May 2013 when it was finally disclosed, some nine months after it actually occurred.

A woman in Southwest Oregon's Josephine County was brutally attacked and sexually assaulted by an ex-boyfriend after she had called the local sheriff's department for help that never came. When the woman was on the telephone with a sheriff's dispatcher, she was told matter-of-factly that nobody was on duty. This was because of budget cuts that resulted in layoffs of 80 percent of the commissioned deputies in the agency.

What happened during this call became a headline of its own, thanks to a transcription of the conversation by National Public Radio. The police dispatcher tells the frantic woman, "You know, obviously if he comes inside the residence and assaults you, can you ask him to go away? Or do you know if he's intoxicated or anything?"

The perpetrator in this event, identified as Michael Bellah, was later apprehended by Oregon State Police. He pleaded guilty to sexual assault and sodomy and was sent to prison.

What happened to the unfortunate woman in Josephine County should not happen to any woman. Gun rights activists might rightly wonder why Bellah is still alive. If the unidentified rape victim had been armed, rather than have had to depend upon sheriff's deputies – none of whom were apparently on duty at the time – state police wouldn't have had to look very hard to find him. Very likely, he would have been found in a pool of blood.

There was something else in the NPR report, a comment by Chris Mallette, who counsels rape and domestic violence victims in Josephine County. She told reporter Amelia Templeton, "The whole system has crumbled and we're the only ones left. And we don't have the badge and we don't have the gun."

Thanks to the gun laws in Oregon, women can remedy half of that problem right away and then get a license to carry.

The story got the attention of Megyn Kelly, a Fox News reporter and anchor who discussed the case on air with regular Fox News contributors Monica Crowley, a conservative author and radio and television commentator, and Sally Kohn, an anti-gun liberal and founder of Movement Vision Lab.

It was this discussion that got writer Sweeney's attention, and provided a text book example of the Left's hypocrisy on women and guns. Here's how Sweeney couched it:

"The debate followed some interesting and predictable paths," he wrote, "the conservative Crowley lamenting the fact that the victim didn't have a gun for self-protection with the liberal Kohn lamenting the fact that government wasn't big enough to protect her.

"As this argument was heating up I said to my co-worker Angi, 'Wait for it, Kohn is going to say if the victim had a gun it would have been used against her'," Sweeney continued.

"Sure enough, when Kohn's turn to speak came up," he detailed, "she stumbled about something then fell back on the well-worn and oft used line 'If the victim had a gun it would probably have been used to kill her.' She then went on to spout off some factoid about homicides in which a gun is used to murder females. I'm pretty certain that she made it up as she went along.

"Raising my hands victoriously I said, 'There it is, the same old argument'," Sweeney reported.

Sweeney was right. The fallback argument of anti-gunners is that women are foolish to have a gun because the larger attackers will take it from them and kill them. It is an argument so demonstrably untrue that it is shocking to see gun prohibitionists continually fall back on it as they try to convince women to remain unarmed.

This is the real "war on women" to which the SAF/CCRKBA video refers; the war that the Left vehemently denies by insisting that their political assault during the 2012 campaign – when they launched the "war on women" strategy to demonize conservatives – was all about abortion and "choice."

Isn't that what self-defense is all about, the right of women to choose whether they will own a gun and defend themselves against an attacker, rather than "ask him to leave?"

This is where Sweeney made his argument so well.

"It never ceases to amaze me how anti-gun liberals will let their overt dislike for firearms and our Second Amendment Civil Rights make them look like idiots and hypocrites," he wrote. "The crowd which has over the decades weaponized the term 'Pro-Choice' in order to derail a long line of conservative candidates has at the same time lost all touch of what and how the 'choice' should apply to.

"Apparently," he concluded, "in liberal fantasy world a woman should have no choice when it comes to their own self-defense and that is just plain wrong. Being a woman who champions liberal causes and at the same time disrespects the capabilities of women is even more so."

Possibly the most startling thing to emerge from this debate were the alternative defense strategies recommended for women who are attacked.

Women who are being attacked, they suggested, should try to vomit or urinate – anything that might be revolting to an attacker bent on violent sexual assault – or even tell the would-be rapist that they are menstruating or suffer from some sexually transmitted disease.

But the idea of having a firearm for personal defense seems more revolting to anti-gunners than the thought of being raped.

Invariably though all of these alternative defenses strategies have a common denominator: The victim must be in physical contact with her attacker.

Only the defensive use of a firearm allows someone to put some distance between themselves and one or more attackers, and maintain that distance, either with the visible threat of lethal force, or its actual use. Once a shot is fired, things can change dramatically in favor of the armed victim, yet another thing the anti-gun lobby refuses to acknowledge.

Not only does this apply to the national gun control debate, it also applies to the international gun control battle, epitomized by the United Nations' Arms Trade Treaty, which was vigorously opposed by every gun rights organization in the country, and by the International Association for the Protection of Civilian Arms Rights (IAPCAR).

Speaking to a UN committee, Julianne Versnel, operations director of the Second Amendment Foundation, noted that "The right of self-defense is a right that is particularly important to women."

"We have a right to protect our bodies, to protect ourselves against assault and rape," she explained. "No one questions that violence against women is endemic. There are those who say women should rely on the police, the authorities, or even the UN for protection. I reject this idea. In fact, this concept is part of the outmoded and disproved idea that women are somehow weaker and must rely on men for their protection.

"Most of the delegates know that in the U.S. there is extensive firearms ownership," she reminded the delegates. "What they do not know is that almost half of the handguns in the U.S. are owned by women. They are used for self-defense by women. I fully endorse, as should every person in this room, the idea that women must have the means to defend themselves. Nothing that is before this Committee…should affect a women's right to defend herself."

Versnel recalled the late Eleanor Roosevelt's travels through the South to defend integration in 1958. The former First Lady carried a .38-caliber revolver after being advised by the Secret Service against making the trip.

"No one supported the UN more than she did," Versnel said, "but at the same time she insisted on her right, as a woman and as a person, to have the means to defend herself."

Would the Left savage Eleanor Roosevelt today? She would probably be told to forego carrying a gun and hire someone else who does carry one to protect her.

CHAPTER 5

AMERICANS HAVE PRIVACY RIGHTS, UNLESS THEY ARE GUN OWNERS

When news agencies began reporting that the National Security Agency (NSA) was collecting telephone records on millions of American citizens, it sent something of a shock wave across the landscape, alarming the public about their privacy from an increasingly prying government.

One other thing this revelation did was provide a graphic, dramatic and immediately understandable reason why so many law-abiding American gun owners have been and remain resistant to invasive background checks. It was eerily noteworthy that this report surfaced almost 64 years to the date that George Orwell's novel *1984* was published. The title of that story, about a totalitarian world in which there was no privacy and "Big Brother" was "watching you," has become as much a part of the American lexicon as *Catch 22*, the title of a Joseph Heller novel about the insanity of war and military regulations.

The British newspaper *The Guardian* broke the story, noting, "The secret Foreign Intelligence Surveillance Court (FISA) granted the order to the FBI on April 25, giving the government unlimited authority to obtain the data for a specified three-month period ending on July 19."

Within days, the report ignited a separate controversy when a former NSA contractor named Edward Snowden was revealed as the source of the story. At first heralded as a whistleblower, he was subsequently branded a traitor by critics of his actions who supported NSA efforts to find terrorists and prevent them from carrying out an attack on United States soil.

The Snowden flap exploded barely two weeks after it was learned that the Justice Department under Attorney General Eric Holder had wrongly branded Fox News correspondent James Rosen as a possible suspect in a criminal case that also involved reporting confidential information. That report came on the heels of revelations that the government had also been snooping into the telephone records of more than 20 Associated Press reporters.

And to top it all off, those revelations surfaced almost simultaneously with reports that the Internal Revenue Service had systematically subjected conservative organizations to special scrutiny, and had delayed their applications for tax-exempt status, while at the same time had been routinely clearing liberal groups for such status.

While the national press corps was fuming about government snooping into their activities, and launching new investigations into prying by the federal government, it universally escaped their attention that they were being subjected to the same kind of scrutiny that gun owners have faced for several years, simply to exercise a constitutionally-protected fundamental civil right. This scrutiny is known as the "instant background check," a process that many in the firearms community consider to be an invasion of privacy, and evidence that gun owners are considered guilty until proven innocent. It could be compared to prior restraint, a term journalists recognize and revile.

Firearms rights activists also argue that the right to keep and bear arms is the only right delineated in the Bill of Rights that citizens must first get permission from the government before they can legally exercise it.

Things were not always this way, but in 1993, when the first Clinton administration worked closely with the Democrat-controlled Congress to pass the Brady Handgun Law, the background check was offered as an alternative to what would have been a national waiting period. The National Rifle Association used the background check to derail the more onerous waiting period measure.

Built into that law were exemptions for private transactions, loans of firearms between family and friends, and gifting of firearms. That was not good enough for gun prohibitionists, who wanted every transaction to require a background check, and for records to be kept on all of those transfers.

This would have amounted to the creation of a *de facto* national gun registry, according to critics in the firearms community, and they fought the idea bitterly.

Perhaps not so remarkably, many of the strongest advocates for gun owner background checks and even more restrictive licensing and registration schemes were also vocal supporters of "motor voter" and other shaky devices that many believed were designed to allow massive voter fraud to the benefit of one political party: Democrats.

Other efforts by anti-gunners have included adoption of ordinances prohibiting background checks on job applicants who might have criminal records, but who are ostensibly looking to start over and turn their lives around. Seattle, Washington provided an example of this moral hypocrisy when the liberal city council adopted just such an ordinance.

They have also opposed voter identification laws, a very contradictory position, because if one must show identification to exercise one constitutional right, then identification should be required to exercise another right, and vice versa.

Likewise, so-called "sanctuary laws" that prohibit local law enforcement from routinely checking the citizenship status of people contacted for everything from traffic stops to criminal investigations also reveal a double standard practiced by the liberal Left.

This drive for background checks on gun buyers is presented as a means of preventing criminals from buying firearms at gun shops and gun shows, but there is an underlying hope on the part of some in the gun prohibition movement that it will discourage potential buyers altogether.

Early in 2013, as President Obama revealed that arms and equipment were being offered to Syrian "rebels," many in the American firearms community wondered if these guns were being "transferred without background checks."

Pry, and pry some more

Gun prohibitionists are fond of accusing firearms owners of being part of a paranoid class, yet when one examines how the gun control lobby continually pursues legislation requiring increasingly invasive background checks, insisting that these intrusions are merely to prevent criminals and crazy persons from accessing firearms, it raises legitimate questions about who the real paranoids are.

Why, for example, should a father be required to go through a background check in order to receive a gift from a son or daughter, or vice versa? Why should someone demand a background check for one hunter to merely loan a firearm to another hunter for a weekend hunting trip?

The purpose of an "instant" background check is to reduce inconvenience to law-abiding citizens who are exercising their civil right to keep and bear arms. The purpose of complicated check requirements and delays is to discourage firearms ownership, just the same as a requirement to obtain a permit to even purchase a firearm.

Ironically, some of the more insidious gun control schemes do not raise alarms with the general public, but that sentiment could gradually change in the wake of government snooping scandals.

What should the "ideal" background check encompass?

That is a question with as many answers as there are individual firearms owners, and they would range from "no background checks, period" to "name, address, date-of-birth and social security number" and nothing more.

It may be of questionable relevance for the background check document to ask whether one is "Hispanic" or "Non-Hispanic," or what other race one happens to be. Regardless of a citizen's heritage, if that individual has a clean record that really is all that should count.

During the height of the National Security Agency domestic telephone records spying flap, the British newspaper *The Guardian* quoted Cato Institute surveillance expert Julian Sanchez, who observed, "We've certainly seen the government increasingly strain the bounds of 'relevance' to collect large numbers of records at once — everyone at one or two degrees of separation from a target — but vacuuming all metadata up indiscriminately would be an extraordinary repudiation of any pretense of constraint or particularized suspicion."

The federal Form 4473 that gun buyers must fill out asks questions about criminal and mental background. Presumably, these questions are aimed at possibly catching someone in a prevarication, but prosecutions for providing false information – unless one is an active straw buyer involved in illegal gun trafficking – are rare.

The NICS database is continually updated, and efforts are underway to add more information about mental health and other "disabilities" that can prevent an individual from buying a firearm. With every new piece of legislation, it seems the goal is to disqualify as many people as possible from buying and owning guns.

When the Senate was debating a so-called "universal background check" measure in early 2013 as a response to the Newtown tragedy, one proposal was to keep records on background checks. Gun rights advocates quickly saw that as a de facto registration scheme, and moved to defeat it.

Such efforts frequently surface in Congress or at the state legislative level, where anti-gun-rights lawmakers evidently believe that the identities of every firearms owner should be in a database. Various conservative commentators have observed that there are "only two reasons for gun registration, to tax them or to take them." That logic is not lost on gun owners, who have seen the kinds of abuses that citizens have experienced in California and elsewhere.

In other countries, owning a firearm is a heavily-regulated privilege that sometimes requires references from at least two people who are not relatives before a person can legally obtain a firearm. Gun owners – especially those in the Western United States – believe this is the kind of regulatory scheme that the gun prohibition lobby would like to see adopted in this country, again as a means of discouraging people from exercising their constitutionally-protected civil right, and micro-managing those who already own firearms.

Indeed, following the United States Supreme Court's 7-2 ruling in June 2013 that overturned an Arizona statute requiring proof of citizenship to vote, some gun owners wondered why there is a double standard on the exercise of gun rights as opposed to voting rights.

Do as I say, not as I do

Innumerable reports over the years about wealthy people and celebrities getting preferential treatment when it comes to carry permits in some jurisdictions often note that the individual involved has supported myriad gun controls for average citizens.

Taking things a step farther, Washington State-based anti-gunner Heidi Yewman, the self-confessed board member of the Brady Campaign and "lead gun policy protester at the 2010 Starbucks' shareholder meeting" over its policy of not banning people who open carry where local laws allow, engaged in some dangerous hypocrisy in mid-2013 when she bought her own handgun and began carrying it, admitting at the time she had no fundamental gun safety or gun handling skills.

According to her blog, appearing on the *Ms. Magazine* website, Yewman bought the 9mm Glock handgun from a local dealer near her home in Vancouver, Wash., and – incredulously, according to several gun owners who read her columns – she walked out of the shop without having been advised about the pistol's operation.

She complained that getting a Washington State concealed pistol license (CPL) "was simple."

"I filled out a form," she explained, "had my fingerprints taken for a background check and paid $56.50. No training required. It took far longer to get my dog a license."

She later explains that it should have been "obvious from the way I handled the gun that I knew nothing about firearms" to the dealer, but he sold it to her, anyway. Well, she passed a background check, which she said took seven minutes.

"Holy hell, that was EASY. Too easy," she reported as though she were gasping for breath from shock.

Then Yewman confessed to two things that gun rights activists in the Pacific Northwest quickly deemed were monumentally foolish. She first stopped on the road where a police officer was conducting an unrelated traffic stop, and told the officer she had just bought the gun and "had no clue how to use it."

"The cop thought I was an idiot," she wrote – a judgment with which gun owners quickly concurred – and added that he "suggested I take a class."

She also contended that she had done nothing illegal, nothing wrong. But blogger Herschel Smith, writing on *The Captain's Journal* in mid-2013, disagreed.

"On the contrary," Smith observed. "She's done everything wrong, from refusing to get adequate training on her firearm and the laws of her state, to asking a cop about anything.

"The drama is exhausting and breathtaking," he continued. "But the thing that really worries me isn't that she has a gun." No, Smith's concern is that people like Yewman "can purchase an SUV the size and weight of my Ford F150 and drive it down the road with screaming kids in the back whilst jabbering on the cell phone attached to her ear, after qualifying with a driving test that a monkey could be trained to take.

"Makes you stop and ponder, no? It's one reason I drive so defensively on the road nowadays," Smith said.

Yewman carried her new gun to a local coffee shop, again without a functional knowledge about how the pistol operated.

Yewman also lamented that in March 2010, she was "surrounded by big hairy men with guns on their hips, yelling at me as I led a protest against Starbuck's (sic) gun policy...Now I'm the one with a gun on her hip. The gun makes me more fearful than I could have imagined."

Where Yewman wants armed citizens to be more responsible, she made it abundantly clear that her own actions were irresponsible. Evidently, that was okay so long as she was trying to prove a point, but it is not entirely clear what point she was making.

First, the National Instant Background Check system functioned as it was supposed to, allowing her to purchase a firearm over the course of just a few minutes because her background checked clear. What other hoops would she advocate for a law-abiding citizen to jump through in order to exercise a fundamental civil right protected by the U.S. and Washington State constitutions?

Second, she obtained her state CPL, again after having cleared a background check. That is the way it is supposed to work under current state statute in Washington, which has had a shall-issue law on the books for more than 30 years.

That her own fear of firearms – a condition defined as "hoplophobia," which is an unnatural fear of firearms – was making her nervous when she was legally armed was a signal, which she ignored, that she was neither ready nor willing to accept the responsibility of carrying a handgun in public.

Yewman's exercise was instructional, but not for the reasons she might have wanted the public to accept. She clearly transferred her personal lack of knowledge and fear of firearms to everyone else who responsibly owns a firearm and carries it regularly. A majority of those people have some experience and training, they have taken the precaution of learning how their gun functions and they do not carry carelessly.

By no small coincidence, this story unfolded about the same time that the Seattle City Council adopted a new hiring regulation that prohibited employment background checks that might wrongly prevent felons from getting jobs in the city.

While her experience was in Washington State, Yewman should know that other jurisdictions are far more complicated – make that discouraging – for the average gun owner or would-be owner. One of the more restrictive states is New York, where new laws have been imposed that have infuriated Empire State gun owners.

Application costs are expensive, and the application allows authorities to obtain sealed criminal records, get complete arrest histories from applicants, and require a Certificate of Disposition on each offense. There is a training requirement, and it can take several months for the process.

Authorities can look at an applicant's driving record, as well.

Many anti-gunners – especially self-righteous newspaper editors who insist on publishing rosters of citizens with concealed carry permits or licenses in their coverage area – do not believe law-abiding gun owners have privacy rights, or at least their rights are subordinate to the right of other people to know who in their neighborhoods own guns.

This situation was brought to the public forum vividly following the Sandy Hook Elementary massacre in late 2012 and early 2013 by the *New York Journal News*. In reaction to the school shooting, it published an interactive map showing the names and addresses of every person with a gun permit in Westchester and Rockland counties. Unfortunately for the newspapers, one of those people happened to be Fox News legal analyst Jeanine Pirro, host of that network's "Justice with Judge Janine." Pirro is a former prosecutor and judge who is known for directness and a no-nonsense attitude.

She pounced on the newspaper's outing of gun permit holders, and the public outrage that followed resulted in adoption of a gun owner privacy tenet to the state's new gun law, adopted in 2013.

The New York case is hardly the only example of media attempts to identify gun owners in what many believe are attempts to subject those citizens to public scorn. Newspapers in Ohio have done the same thing at various times over the years, insisting that publishing what amounts to a road map for burglars to the homes of gun owners is socially justifiable.

It was with no small amount of irony that the *Columbus Dispatch* criticized the *New York Journal News* for what essentially was a publicity stunt. Noting that "without any compelling reason nor any purpose that benefits the public, the Journal News was wrong – and foolish – to invade the privacy of so many people."

When newspapers go at one another, there is ample reason to believe that one of the newspapers did something very wrong, because newspapers do not characteristically criticize one another over trivial things. The *Columbus Dispatch* made clear which newspaper in this case was the culprit. The *Dispatch* rightly wondered, "In what way is the fact that Joe Smith of 123 Maple St. has a gun permit relevant to the awful tragedy at Sandy Hook Elementary in Newtown, Conn.? Did the paper mean to suggest a connection between those presumably law-abiding gun owners and the deranged Adam Lanza's carnage? Surely it didn't, but the outrage of gun owners and those who feel strongly about gun rights is understandable. And what the paper did mean to convey is impossible to discern."

So rare is this kind of criticism by one newspaper against the actions of another that it merits recognition and discussion. More typically, newspapers copycat one another with this kind of outing-the-gun-owners escapade. It is designed to gin up reader numbers through sensationalism, rather than something truly tangible.

As the *Dispatch* observed, "If the Journal News had compared the list of gun-permit holders to a database of felony offenders and found that permits were given to felons, or if it found that those with personal or political connections were given special access to permits, that would have justified naming some permit holders. If analysis showed a meaningful connection between gun-ownership rates and high or low crime, that could justify mapping the locations of permit holders, though their names would be irrelevant."

But there is more at work here than merely ramping up publicity. There was strong concern at the time that what the New York newspaper did was vindictive. As noted above, this exercise had something of a nasty taint to it; an effort to publicly embarrass gun owners in the two counties, and perhaps even discourage someone else from owning a firearm out of fear of public exposure.

If that was an accurate assessment of the *Journal News'* purpose, it crossed the line so far that had the story to do with subject other than gun ownership, a reporter and editor might have been disciplined for injecting personal bias into what was supposed to be straight news.

Bad medicine?

Florida provided the country with some interesting examples of what can happen when the medical community tries to exert its influence into the firearms rights debate.

There may be no greater privacy issue than that involving an individual's personal health, and while the controversy we are about to discuss involves what happened in Florida, this is really a cause that has affected firearms owners across the United States. A person must be able to trust their physician, so when a doctor begins asking questions about a subject for which he or she has no visible training – firearms safety – other than what may have been written in some medical journal by another doctor who had no hands-on experience, much less expertise, with firearms, it creates a huge problem.

Florida citizens fought over the issue of physicians inquiring about firearms in the homes, a subject that firearms owners, and the National Rifle Association, argued was beyond the scope of a medical doctor – what the medical community considers a "boundary violation" when it is a subject that is not related to the health of a patient – unless that doctor happens to be a certified firearms instructor.

Anti-gunners in the medical community have long contended, with not much other than opinion to support their assertion – that "gun violence" is a public health issue. It is as though they had to invent some reason to get involved in the firearms rights debate, an area of public policy into which they should not stick their stethoscope.

That issue wound its way through the courts after legislation, dubbed the Firearm Owners Privacy Act was passed to prohibit physicians from discussing guns with their patients, was challenged. In mid-2012, a federal judge blocked the state from enforcing the law, which forbade doctors from talking to patients about gun ownership. U.S. District Judge Marcia Cooke said the statute violated the doctors' First Amendment rights.

However, in July 2014, a panel of judges on the U.S. Court of Appeals for the 11th Circuit upheld the statute. The court panel said the law was a "legitimate regulation of professional conduct." The case could have far-reaching ramifications beyond the Florida borders.

Gun owners were incensed that their family doctor might be encouraged to inquire whether there were firearms in their homes, and how they might be stored. That kind of information is none of a doctor's business unless it has some direct bearing on a health issue, say firearms rights advocates. This is where the gun control crowd promotes the theory that people with emotional troubles might be dangerous to themselves if there are firearms in the home and they are easily accessible.

Narrowing the scope of the debate in the aftermath of Sandy Hook, gun prohibitionists and gun rights activists also tangled over legislation to prevent people from buying firearms if they have mental health issues. The legislation, according to WJXT News, required people who voluntarily underwent mental health screening to surrender their firearms rights.

The bill had bipartisan support in the legislature but instead of the firearms community resisting, opposition came from mental health professionals. Their spokesperson, John Bryant, representing the Florida Council for Community Mental Health, contended that a federal standard, rather than one established by the state, should take precedence.

Published reports said that mental health professionals resisted the measure on the argument that fewer people – translate that to firearms owners – would seek treatment for mental disorders if they knew doing so would cost them their gun rights.

It created something of a paradox for the mental health community because on the one hand, they want people with mental health problems to be disarmed and prevented from buying more guns, while at the same time arguing that such laws discourage people from seeking treatment because of a guaranteed loss of Second Amendment rights.

That is more than just a right wing fantasy, as there are countless cases of military veterans losing their gun rights over treatment for post-traumatic stress disorders following their return from the Middle East. Conversely, there is no way to tell how many others have rejected treatment because of those concerns.

Incredibly, the Obama administration found itself on the "wrong" side in this dilemma when the White House began pushing for an expanded National Instant Check System (NICS) database that includes the names of more mental patients who may be disqualified from owning firearms.

Alienating one of his strongest voting blocs – the medical community – President Obama in 2013 launched various efforts under executive actions including one to make more states to add the names. But the mental health community became furious fast. In the process, the administration moved to change rules regarding the privacy of health information under the Health Insurance Portability and Accountability Act (HIPAA). Leading mental health professionals demonized the effort, among them Massachusetts psychiatrist Daniel Fisher, who had once been treated for schizophrenia.

Quoted by Reuters, Dr. Fisher was blunt: "I think it's a bad idea. It would really put a chill on people getting services."

Chiming in from the other corner was Lindsay Nichols, an attorney – another one of Barack Obama's core support professions – who works at the Law Center to Prevent Gun Violence. She said a change in the HIPAA law would give state officials cover for turning over mental health records to the NICS system.

"This action," she told Reuters, "would eliminate the excuse which is used by legislators and other officials for not reporting information to NICS."

Ironically, in the process of debating the anti-gun president's recommendation, mental health professionals defined one of the major reasons law-abiding gun owners are concerned and even fearful of expanded background checks and other government intrusions into their exercise of their Second Amendment rights.

"I don't think of myself as at all paranoid about this, but I do think that a lot of people worry that information may not be as secure as we all want to be reassured that it is," said James Jackson, executive director of Disability Rights New Mexico, according to Reuters' lengthy exploration of the issue.

Policy analyst Marilyn Martin, with the Chicago-based Access Living group, observed that, "The constant chronic coupling of gun violence with mental illness is just devastating."

What about the much more malignant, and broader, "chronic coupling" of all criminal violence involving firearms with the millions of law-abiding gun owners who were not connected with the crimes, but have been demonized and penalized all the same as a result of those crimes? The press all too frequently plays fast and loose with facts and public emotion when covering gun-related crimes. There was a considerable amount of misinformation following the Sandy Hook tragedy and even the Boston Marathon. Nobody has ever apologized to gun owners for the bad rap they took, as a social group, from negative coverage of the horrific events.

What these cases demonstrate is that the gun control debate is like a magnet for anti-gunners to use whatever reasoning that appears rational to inject themselves and their opinions, while at the same time insisting on a hands-off approach when it comes to their own pet areas and issues.

In the process, the privacy of gun-owning patients is easily compromised as anti-gunners in the medical and psychiatric professions place their partisanship ahead of the interests of their patients.

One organization we mentioned earlier, Doctors for Responsible Gun Ownership, has provided some powerful arguments against this sort of anti-gun lobbying disguised as health care. Dr. Timothy Wheeler, who founded and still heads this project, has had numerous articles and opinion pieces published, detailing why the medical community should steer clear of this politically-charged morass.

A stickler for accuracy, Wheeler has also appeared at several Gun Rights Policy Conference events. The GRPC annually brings together a veritable Who's Who in the gun rights community, and Wheeler's discussions have been eye-openers for audiences all over the map.

DRGO is a national organization, with some 1,400 medical doctors and other health care professionals among its members. Wheeler founded the organization in 1994, when being a pro-gun Southern California surgeon might not have been considered the safest career move.

But Wheeler was determined that the "other side" of the guns-and-medicine argument be heard, and for two decades, he's been on the leading edge of this debate.

Originally a project of the Claremont Institute, a California think tank, DRGO was adopted by the Second Amendment Foundation in 2011 and continues as an alternative voice to the gun prohibition movement within the medical community. While DRGO has not quelled the anti-gun rhetoric from some medical professionals, it has certainly put the political physicians on notice that they are being watched and that they have "competition."

You're on Candid Android

Even more alarming, if not downright sinister in the scheme of privacy invasion was the announcement of a new Android app that would have its users strolling around their neighborhoods with the intention of "exposing" the home addresses of gun owners, especially those they believe are "potentially unsafe."

Before anyone thinks this is nonsense, the Gun Geo Marker was released to Google's Play app store in early July 2013. At the time, it was widely reported that the app "allows users to add detailed locations of possible gun owners or gun-owning businesses to a map database" according to one report in *Field & Stream* magazine.

Reviewers seemed split on the idea, with one suggesting that it is "a major invasion of privacy" and another arguing that it is "dangerous and invasive." On the other side, Brett Stalbaum, identified by Fox News as the developer of the Gun Geo Marker, alleged that "The gun rights community has been busy making personal threats…as well as spamming the Gun Geo Marker database with false markers."

He was quoted as stating that, "This kind of reaction – automatically lining up on the wrong side of reasonable measures to improve the safe use and ownership of guns – aids and abets the crisis of child shooting deaths."

But researcher and author John Lott, whose book More *Guns = Less Crime* became a ground breaking look at firearms ownership in America and how it correlates with lower crime rates, said the safety issue is really with the app making it easier for criminals to target unarmed homes.

'I've debated a lot of gun control advocates over the years," he said in an interview, "and I've never met someone who has been willing to put up a sign in front of their house indicating that their home is a gun-free zone."

Stalbaum said in his Fox News interview that he is a gun owner.

"I want to see our rights preserved," he stated, "and thwarting the will of 90 percent of the American people who want common sense, constitutional measures to improve gun safety is mathematically unwise."

But where in the constitution does it say that the homes of gun owners may be targeted by someone with an Android device and identified as a potential threat to the community? And what poll says 90 percent of the American public is in favor of such an invasion of privacy?

Obama administration hypocrisy

Emily Miller, the award-winning former senior opinion editor at the *Washington Times* and now chief investigative reporter with the Fox News affiliate in Washington, D.C., brought up another interesting aspect of the privacy controversy when she did a column that discussed federal lawsuits filed by the Equal Employment Opportunity Commission (EEOC) against two companies, Dollar General in Illinois and BMW in South Carolina. The lawsuits asserted that both companies violated the 1964 Civil Rights Act by using criminal background checks to decide whether to employ a job applicant.

Perhaps coincidentally, about that same time, the anti-gun administration of former Seattle, Wash., Mayor Mike McGinn decided that criminal background checks would no longer be used in hiring employees for some jobs in the city.

But this seemed like a double standard to Miller, who very pointedly raised the issue in a column in which she led off with this line: "Not wanting to employ a criminal makes you a racist." She subsequently took a hard look at the EEOC complaints, and determined that there was a double standard at work.

"The Obama administration's feel-good liberalism and political correctness override common sense and public safety," Miller wrote. "The policy could mean that child care workers and teachers cannot be given background checks, leaving the possibility that rapists and child molesters would not be screened out of the jobs.

"More broadly," she continued, "it also may be racial discrimination to conduct FBI background checks for felony records before selling firearms because that, too, would turn up a higher percentage of minorities than whites."

This is not merely provocative hyperbole, but a serious issue.

Miller noted that "blacks and Hispanics have significantly higher rates of incarceration than whites."

This may be a sad commentary on the justice system, or it might be a terrible signal that there is something very wrong in the minority community, whether it is lack of parental discipline, lack of parental guidance due to a high rate of out-of-wedlock pregnancies, or any combination of factors including economic and educational disadvantages. However, suggesting that running background checks on job applicants who may have criminal convictions is racist – while endorsing criminal background checks on all prospective gun owners – becomes somewhat twisted in logic.

The Obama administration moved to quash the practice of conducting background checks for a criminal history for sensitive jobs that may involve children or other sensitive business, yet the same administration is perfectly comfortable with the notion that background checks must be conducted on all firearms transactions, even for citizens who possess concealed carry licenses or permits, a document that is not issued unless the recipient first passes a background check.

It is an exercise in hypocrisy that means honest firearms owners and buyers need to be checked, but those with a criminal background do not. What is wrong with that picture? Miller's probing sought the answer.

"When someone has committed a crime, he must take responsibility for it, and if that means losing a job to someone who has led a law-abiding life, so be it."

The EEOC flap occurred at the same time President Obama was advocating wider access to mental health records, suggesting an even higher degree of hypocrisy. If, as mental health proponents have insisted, the majority of mentally ill people are no threat to anybody and should not have their medical records accessible to a snoopy government, then why would the administration want to invade their privacy while protecting the privacy of convicted criminals?

Taken as a whole, the controversy over privacy rights versus public safety has made for some strange political parallels, and the firearms community – with its objections to expanded and invasive background checks and their possible misuse to create de facto gun registries – has been far more consistent than those on the anti-gun Left, which can't decide whether it likes checks or doesn't like them, depending upon who is being targeted.

CHAPTER 6
HOW CRIMINALS, TERRORISTS BECOME 'GUN VIOLENCE' VICTIMS

When billionaire anti-gun former New York Mayor Michael Bloomberg launched a 25-state, 100-city gun control bus tour that ostensibly memorialized the victims of "gun violence," he and the Mayors Against Illegal Guns (MAIG) that he founded and funded ended up with egg on their collective face.

Among the names of the dead that were initially read aloud at these staged media events were the suspected Boston Marathon bomber, Tamerlan Tsarnaev, and a few criminals who had been shot by police or private citizens in self-defense.

At the time, coauthor Alan Gottlieb issued a bristling statement to the press, condemning the inclusion of those names.

"This is so far beyond insulting, I'm not sure there's a word in the dictionary to describe it," he said. "It clearly demonstrates that Michael Bloomberg's gun prohibition effort will exploit even the names of dead terror suspects to further his anti-gun agenda. That's a new low that I didn't think was possible."

Among the other names were Christopher Dorner, the California ex-cop who allegedly murdered another police officer and was the subject of an intense man hunt before he was killed in a fire following a shootout, and Jeremy Peter Goulet, killed in Santa Cruz, Calif., after he allegedly gunned down two police detectives.

Also on the list were:

- Esteban J. Smith, suspected of the stabbing death of his wife, who was killed by Elden, Tex., police after what was described as a "shooting rampage."

- Would-be cop-killer Kurt Myers, who was shot by his intended police victims in Herkimer, N.Y. He allegedly murdered four people the day before lawmen took him down.

- Rick Odell Smith, killed by police in Manchester, Ill. after allegedly shooting six people with a shotgun.

- Murder suspects Emmanuel Gatewood and Kourtney Hahn, who died in a gun battle with police in Columbus, Ohio.

- Another Ohio outlaw, James L. Gilkerson, killed in a Middlefield shootout with police.

- Anthony James Galla, killed by cops in Upper Darby, Pa., ending a manhunt that began with another shooting.

Eventually, according to one account, a review of 617 killings found that 50 were suspects in crimes ranging from assault to murder, not the type of violence Bloomberg's group suggests in its "No More Names" campaign to draw attention to the estimated 6,000 gun death "tragedies" that were tallied during the months following mid-December 2012 Sandy Hook Elementary School shooting.

Paul Bedard at the *Washington Examiner* reported that when the list of Montana gun victims was analyzed on its own more than half of those people named had either committed suicide or were shot by police.

The anti-gun mayors' group scrambled to do damage control. In the process, it revealed that the list of names had come from Slate, whose editor, Dan Kois, admitted to *The Atlantic Wire* that the Tsarnaev's name was intentionally included on the list of "gun victims." His explanation for that was curious to say the least.

"The interactive is a tally of all the people who've been killed by guns since the Newtown shootings," he was quoted as stating. "So it doesn't differentiate between good guys and bad guys. We were studiously attempting to be as clear as possible that this was not victims of gun crimes ... it was everybody that's been killed by guns since Newtown."

Nobody is killed "by" a gun, but by someone using the gun, the same as no one is killed by a hammer, rock, club or baseball bat. That probably didn't matter to Kois because, as he explained it to *The Atlantic Wire*, the fact that Tsarnaev may have been run over by his brother before or after being shot by police makes him a gunshot victim.

"For the purposes of this interactive," he explained, 'killed-by-gun-plus-other-thing counts."

The incident set off a huge negative public reaction that was so bad, the Mayors Against Illegal Guns was compelled to issue a public apology.

"The names of victims since the Newtown tragedy are being read by survivors and others to show the very real and personal cost of gun violence," MAIG said in a press release. "A small number of names on the public list compiled by *Slate.com* entitled 'How Many People Have Been Killed by Guns Since Newtown?' have been of people who were absolutely not victims, which was a mistake that is being corrected, and for which we apologize."

That apology fell on deaf ears, especially in the firearms community.

"If Bloomberg and his Mayors Against Illegal Guns are willing to make a martyr of a terror suspect to push their agenda," Gottlieb said at the time, "it raises questions about the legitimacy of their campaign to disarm America, one legislative step at a time. Next thing you know, they'll be calling Osama bin Laden a victim of gun violence, too."

It has long been suspected, and occasionally demonstrated anecdotally, that the gun prohibition lobby pads its data or at least spins it to create the impression of a disaster when none is there. There have been, over the years, instances when anti-gunners stretched things a bit – for example when "children" are defined as people in their late teens, or when they lump together ten years of data to come up with some sensational number for a body count to exceed some battlefield statistic.

In August 2011, the *Detroit Free Press* reviewed the ten-year history of reformed concealed carry in Michigan. The two-part story contained some blistering information about the gun prohibition lobby that raised more than just a few eyebrows. "The Freep," as it is popularly known, took a hard look at the anti-gun Violence Policy Center's Web page called "Concealed Carry Killers." That page purports to tally the carnage that results when states, such as Michigan, authorize ordinary citizens under most circumstances to be licensed to carry concealed guns.

According to the VPC, citizens who get through the background checks and jump through all of the other bureaucratic hoops to secure a carry permit or license "routinely" kill police officers and perpetrate mass murders. At the time the story was published, the newspaper noted that the VPC had counted 308 "Private Citizens Killed By Concealed Carry Killer" (sic) since 2007. Seventy-eight of them were Michiganers.

But the newspaper said that a closer look at VPC's data did not necessarily confirm a CCW crime nightmare scenario. The overwhelming majority of Michigan victims the center cited (62) were licensees who committed suicide. Michigan's concealed weapons law requires the State Police to report annually on deaths by suicide of license holders.

Suicide typically occurs in a place and under a set of circumstances that have nothing at all to do with concealed carry. Whether the victim had a carry license is thus irrelevant...except, apparently, to the VPC in its effort to jack up the numbers.

The newspaper lamented that the VPC's reports contained no information about how the licensee died or whether a firearm was involved in the actual suicide.

But here's where things got interesting: Several other gun violence "victims" in the VPC report appear to have been criminals who were killed by legally-armed citizens during the course of a robbery or other felony.

"But with 276,000 concealed pistol license holders, even the un-scrubbed VPC numbers hardly establish evidence of a crime wave," the newspaper observed.

Is that not what legal concealed carry is all about? Is this not the purpose that lies at the foundation of concealed carry by law-abiding citizens who have taken responsibility for their own safety? The shooters in these cases defended themselves and possibly others by using their legally-carried guns to stop a threat in progress. Even the president of the state's association of county prosecutors at the time, Ionia County prosecutor Ronald Schafer, had to acknowledge to the newspaper, "I think you can look back and say 'It was a big nothing'." He further admitted, "We were all a little too caught up imagining what might happen."

Anti-gunners, as history has demonstrated repeatedly, have sometimes very vivid imaginations. In the minds of gun prohibitionists, a dead criminal is a victim, apparently.

Cover boy bomber

This mindset allegedly took a new low turn when *Rolling Stone* ran a photo of Boston Marathon bombing suspect Dzhokhar Tsarnaev on its July 2013 cover. The image drew a furiously negative reaction from readers and commercial backlash from vendors, who refused to place that particular issue on their newsstands.

One might call it a public revulsion that the iconic magazine had "stooped" to running a boyish rock-star style photo of a true public enemy as though he were just some misunderstood teen looking for his place in life.

For several days the controversy unfolded, with *Rolling Stone* suffering the worst of it, though many believe it may have been a circulation stunt designed to boost sales. There are some stunts that should not be attempted, as the negative reaction demonstrated.

What was also demonstrated, however, is how far some in the media have tilted to the left. The same "objective" journalists who glorify criminals and suspected criminals are the same people giving knee jerk approval to every gun control measure to come along.

Eerily, there was a disturbing angle of the Tsarnaev story that did not get the attention it possibly deserved. At the time the magazine article appeared, the bombing suspect had attracted supporters who claimed he and his deceased brother were the victims of profiling and actually were not responsible for the bombing. Tsarnaev was behind bars because of a conspiracy to blame him for a monstrous crime he didn't commit, according to his supporters.

It was reminiscent of a monster from an earlier generation, Theodore Robert Bundy, the cold-blooded serial killer who left a trail of corpses from Washington to Florida. Bundy attracted several female admirers along the way – fortunately for them none ever dated Bundy – who succumbed to his handsome looks, smooth talk and pleas of innocence, right up to the hours before he was electrocuted in Florida for murders to which he confessed, but only in an attempt to barter more time to live. Police investigators described him as "a monster" and there is nothing to suggest otherwise, once the evidence of his heinous crimes was fully revealed.

Bundy and other serial killers didn't shoot their victims. An anomaly to the typical serial killer profile was David Berkowitz, the infamous "Son of Sam," who shot his victims with a .44-caliber revolver. One might argue that since none of the Boston Marathon victims were shot that could explain the appeal Tsarnaev has with some people, including the *Rolling Stone* editors.

The naming of Tsarnaev's brother as a gun violence victim might have gone unnoticed had not some sharp-eared firearms enthusiasts turned out to observe one of the MAIG anti-gun events in New Hampshire. When the name of Tamerlan Tsarnaev was read aloud, people quickly began shouting that "he's a terrorist." That was when things began unraveling for the Bloomberg anti-gun tour.

Embarrassment was immediately evident when organizers of the New Hampshire rally declined to speak to the *New Hampshire Union Leader*. It was not until later that the aforementioned apology was issued.

Had this unfolded a century earlier, one might suspect that the names of Henry McCarty (also known as William Bonney), Clell Miller, William Stiles and the Dalton brothers, Robert Leroy Parker and Harry Alonzo Longabaugh – all Old West outlaws killed during the commission of crimes except for Bonney – might have also been considered victims of "gun violence." Miller and Stiles were members of the James-Younger gang killed by armed citizens during a botched bank robbery in Northfield, Minnesota. Brothers Bob and Grat Dalton, along with Dick Broadwell and Bill Power, were killed by lawmen and armed citizens when they tried to rob two banks simultaneously in Coffeyville, Kansas. Bonney, otherwise known as "Billy the Kid," was shot dead by Sheriff Pat Garrett at Fort Sumner, New Mexico. Parker and Longabaugh were far better known by their respective aliases, Butch Cassidy and the Sundance Kid, and they were apparently killed in South America, though there has long been conjecture that one or the other made it back to the states and lived quietly under another assumed name.

The fact that they were all shot might have been all the excuse needed by Slate to have their names read on a list of gun violence victims, one might presume.

It should be noted that, prior to the Internet and modern gun control movement, outlaws including Bonney, the Daltons, Youngers and James brothers did enjoy a certain degree of popular notoriety. The film about Butch and Sundance became a western classic that glossed over the fact that they made a living by stealing from others, at gunpoint.

But at the end of the day, these men were all criminals, committing robberies and occasionally killing innocent people during the course of their holdups. The Northfield gun battle left several people dead, as did the open street gun battle in Coffeyville. Still, several popular films have been made about these outlaws, leaving audiences with the impression that they really weren't bad guys, when they really were.

'Turning their lives around'

There are so many anecdotal stories about young men who die during the commission of a violent act who are subsequently remembered by friends and family as "just turning his life around" that it could almost be said without tongue-in-cheek that this has become an epidemic contributor to the cause of death, if one were doing a government study, that is.

The press seems to thrive on such stories, and reporters never seem to miss an opportunity to milk one of these cases as a tragedy. In the process, they all-too-often cleanse the backgrounds of people who may have had it coming, particularly people killed during the commission of an armed robbery or some other violent crime.

Indeed, the on-line "Urban Dictionary" discusses this apologist nonsense, noting, "The phrase commonly said by a career criminal's family to the media after getting killed by the police or citizen during the commission of a felonious act. The deceased victim's family will tell tall stories of how the deceased was going to be a sports star or a rapper."

While it seems poor manners to speak ill of the dead, there are occasions when such a death would be surprising if it hadn't occurred. A careful study of the backgrounds of some of these people reveals a self-destructive lifestyle and behavior pattern from which premature death becomes nearly as predictable.

That said, it perhaps becomes understandable amid the grief of losing one's offspring – nobody should live long enough to bury their children – under clearly bad circumstances, one can be afforded a bit of latitude in the selective memory department.

Take the case of Dwayne Atkins, 28, who was found lying in a pool of his own blood in an apartment building hallway. According to the *New Orleans Times-Picayune*, Atkins had been shot several times. His mother told the newspaper that Atkins was "trying to do the right thing and change his lifestyle." Evidently, he didn't change fast enough.

Atkins' lifestyle, by the way, included arrests for drugs and even murder, though the murder charge was later dropped, the newspaper noted.

Then there was a San Diego man identified by the *Union Tribune* newspaper as Angel Miguel Lopez, killed in January 2013. According to his widow, Mr. Lopez "was trying to turn his life around." He apparently didn't try hard enough, because he was shot dead by police in a foot chase after he ran from an apartment complex where he wound up in the middle of a police stakeout. When police ordered him to stop and show his hands, he instead made a motion like he was reaching for a gun in his pocket.

Mr. Lopez had done time for robbery and at the time of his death, he was facing trial on a weapons charge. Months before his demise, he had been arrested on a parole violation for a different beef.

Google the phrase "He was just turning his life around" and one gets more than 443,000,000 possible results. It suggests that in far too many cases, the friends and relatives of a recently departed soul are delusional about the dead person.

Unfortunately, this delusion can creep into the reporting of such slayings. Perhaps part of it can be explained as an attempt by reporters to humanize a person who was killed at an early stage in life and present a picture of someone who had more than a criminal dimension. But in the process, these people become victims rather than the perpetrators they were.

After all, how does one become the "victim" of an armed shopkeeper who shoots them dead rather than be executed so there are no witnesses, or just because some scumbag wanted the thrill of cancelling a life?

Lost frequently in the broader debate is the fact that when one of these typically-teen felons is slain during the course of a criminal act, the press neglects to report that it would have been illegal for them to be carrying a concealed handgun under any circumstances because they are not old enough to qualify for a carry license or permit. Not only might their juvenile criminal background throw up a roadblock, but they simply did not meet the age requirement, typically 21 years.

This should be required reporting for any news agency following one of these sad stories. The public should be constantly reminded that the dead would-be criminal had already broken more than one existing gun law.

Since this is not part of the typical reporting pattern, it becomes easier for gun control advocates to treat these outlaws as victims of "gun violence."

Crime beat reporters should follow up their stories about cancelled lives by inquiring about where the dead criminal got the gun. Teens certainly don't get them from storefront businesses, nor would they get them from gun shows without the cooperation of a straw buyer. Traces almost invariably turn up stolen gun reports, or they come from acquaintances, someone trades other stolen property or drugs, or they are obtained through other illicit means. Occasionally, a stolen gun is traced back to a police officer or some other law enforcement professional.

Ultimately, the issue comes back, or should come back, to the parents. Responsible teens know they cannot be walking around with a concealed handgun because it is illegal and could get them in a great deal of trouble. Responsible teens learn this from responsible parents.

Once in that criminal groove, however, it becomes increasingly difficult to turn one's life around. The misguided sentiment becomes an epitaph.

In self-defense

The oft-repeated lament about how "30,000 people" die each year from "gun violence" breaks down to less than 50 percent being actual crime victims when one analyzes the statistical data. The rest are suicides, accidental deaths and justifiable homicides; that is, killings done in self-defense or the defense of others, or in the case of law enforcement, in the line of duty.

It is not impossible for the public, and especially members of the press, to get some information on the number of justifiable homicides in any given year. This data is found in the FBI's annual Uniform Crime Report, a document that provides probably the most accurate assessment of crime in the United States, and without any political bias. To find it simply use your Internet search engine to look up the Uniform Crime Report, then click on the link to Expanded Offense Data and follow that to Murders and Justifiable Homicides, the latter which are divided into two categories, committed by law enforcement officers and those by private citizens. There are separate tables for each, so it is impossible to get them confused.

Earlier, we noted the FBI Uniform Crime Report data for 2012. What we did not detail were the justifiable homicides included in that report. That year, there were 410 total justifiable killings by law enforcement, of which 409 involved firearms. Of those, 328 were committed with handguns, 36 with rifles and 7 with shotguns. Another 38 did not report the type of firearm used.

In 2011, the FBI reported 393 justifiable law enforcement homicides including 390 committed with firearms. There were 397 justified killings by police in 2010 and 414 in 2009.

Armed private citizens killed 270 people in self-defense in 2011, the majority of which involved handguns (156), while 13 were done with rifles and 11 involved shotguns, and 29 which were not defined. In 2010, armed citizens justifiably killed 285 attackers, and firearms were involved in 236 of those cases, and in 2009 armed citizens accounted for another 266 justifiable homicides of which 218 incidents involved firearms, the FBI report said.

Here are a couple of other significant numbers from the 2012 Uniform Crime Report. There were 518 slayings with "blunt objects" and another 674 that were bare-hand crimes in which someone used his hands and/or feet to kill the victim. Notice that there were more blunt object and bare hands killings than those involving rifles (of all kinds, not just semi-automatics) or shotguns, yet the gun prohibition lobby has been on a crusade to ban so-called "assault weapons" that are primarily recognized as semi-automatic rifles. Why?

Critics of armed self-defense have latched onto another target, the so-called "Stand Your Ground" laws that have been adopted in some 30 states over the past several years, and are specifically singled out in the gun control playbook for demonization as "shoot first" and "kill at will" laws as noted in Chapter One. In the next chapter, we will take a hard look at these statutes in relation to the case that really put these laws in the political spotlight: the shooting of Trayvon Martin by George Zimmerman.

For now, the proposed ban on certain rifles would be a symbolic trophy, one of those "feel good" accomplishments used to raise funds and create the impression that something important and wonderful had been done, when quite the opposite is actually true.

This follows the same logic as easily distorted "crime gun" data. Not all "crime guns" are used in the commission of a crime. Many of these firearms are recovered from burglary arrests, or found by police doing searches for other offenses, but because they are found at crime scenes, they become part of that "crime gun" number, same as a recidivist felon whose criminal career is cut short by an intended victim becomes a victim of "gun violence."

Recovery of semi-autos at crime scenes makes them "crime guns" but not necessarily murder weapons. However, after the gun control lobby pumps out a boilerplate statement that invariably perpetuates the distorted body count, the press all-too-frequently does no follow-up to confirm the information or analyze it.

If they did, they would learn that not all of the homicides were gunshot related anywhere United States. Firearms do account for the majority of homicides, as any expert can confirm, but when gun prohibitionists begin pandering to an unsuspecting public about the number of murders committed annually, some people contend that these homicides by "other means" and suicides are included as "victims of gun violence" to inflate the statistics.

In preparation for this book, a call was made to the Seattle Police Department to get a count on the number of homicides during the first half of 2013. SPD had those numbers, but they included three people who were fatally shot by police. SPD's logical explanation was that they are legally all defined as homicides; therefore they are all lumped together. Presumably, however, when Seattle relays its year-end data to the FBI, those cases are separated.

The number also included two men with criminal backgrounds who were shot dead while sitting in a car, one man who died from a wound suffered in a previous year, and others who were in the wrong place at the wrong time.

But at the end of the day – at the end of their day – the thugs, would-be recidivist criminals and other bad seeds became "victims" by the Bloomberg-MAIG standard.

Go figure.

CHAPTER 7

NOTHING WRONG WITH JUSTICE SO LONG AS YOU CAN LYNCH SOMEONE

George Zimmerman. Trayvon Martin.

The two names are now indelibly and eternally linked in the nation's history and public lexicon, about the same way that injustice and lynch mobs run together. From the moment early news reports revealed that Martin was a black unarmed teen and Zimmerman was something else – it went from white, to Hispanic and finally to a "white Hispanic," whatever that is – the media and professional race hucksters began pandering to their respective audiences about racial profiling, Florida's unpopular-with-liberals Stand Your Ground law, concealed carry and any other subject they could demonize and exploit.

Trayvon Martin was returning to his father's house after visiting a convenience store in suburban Sanford, Florida on the night of Feb. 26, 2012. He was on foot.

George Zimmerman was the neighborhood watch coordinator, or "captain." He was running errands that had nothing to do with his role with the neighborhood watch program. He was not "on duty" that evening, but he was cognizant of the fact that his neighborhood had experienced some recent burglaries. He was armed with a 9mm Kel-Tec semiautomatic pistol.

The 28-year-old Zimmerman spotted Martin, who was wearing a hoodie and walking through the neighborhood in an allegedly suspicious manner. It was dark, and thinking something might be wrong, Zimmerman called the local police to report his observations.

At the time, Zimmerman could not tell the race of the individual he was observing, and that was confirmed in the full recording obtained from the police after the incident; an audio that was edited – some call it "doctored" – by a local NBC affiliate crew that was ultimately dismissed.

There is only one version of the encounter in full, that offered by Zimmerman in the aftermath. Martin was on the phone with a friend at the time, but the call broke off before the actual incident and shooting occurred.

The story has been told and re-told, but the salient facts, which led the jury to hand down a not-guilty verdict in Zimmerman's Second-degree murder trial, were that Zimmerman got out of his car to get more information for the police. Martin had disappeared from his view. When the police call-taker learned Zimmerman was on foot following the suspect, he was told "we don't need you to do that." It was not an order to stop, and it did not have the force of law.

Zimmerman, at that point, broke off his "pursuit" to return to his car, and he was struck by a surprise blow to the face that knocked him down, and Martin was quickly on top of him. Initially, according to all available evidence, Zimmerman was lying on a sidewalk and his head was slammed against the cement.

Martin allegedly spotted Zimmerman's handgun. There was a struggle during which the teen allegedly told the older man that he was "going to die tonight." Zimmerman managed to draw the pistol first and fire the fatal shot.

As with any case, the facts of the Zimmerman-Martin shooting will be debated *ad nauseum* by various experts. Perhaps only one analysis emerges from all the debate and rhetoric, and it comes from a man who, over the past three-plus decades has earned a reputation for crime incident analysis and courtroom expertise: Massad Ayoob, founder of the Lethal Force Institute and more recently operating his own Massad Ayoob Group firearms and self-defense training program.

In a multi-part series on the *Backwoods Home* website, Ayoob did an exhaustive analysis of the evidence and court testimony, and other documentation. Here is how he described how the incident likely unfolded:

"The evidence indicates that Zimmerman didn't get out of his car until the operator asked where the suspicious person was," Ayoob wrote, "and where the police should meet Zimmerman, the complainant. Taking that as a request for information, Zimmerman obligingly got out of the car to gather the intelligence that seemed to have been implicitly requested of him. He was, after all, the elected (not self-appointed) captain of Neighborhood Watch, and his function as Eyes and Ears of the Police had been drilled into him and the other Watch members through the Police Department itself. When the call-taker asked if he was following the man, Zimmerman replied in the affirmative."

It was at that point, according to the evidence and Ayoob's analysis, that Zimmerman was told, 'You don't have to do that'," by the dispatcher.

"The evidence indicates that he stopped following Martin at that moment," Ayoob meticulously reported. "His former rapid breathing returned to normal and wind noise from his phone stopped, consistent with his testimony that he stopped following and had lost sight of Martin. The dispatcher did not 'order' him to stop following, and later admitted in court that he had no authority to do so. Nonetheless, it was clear that Zimmerman was simply following Martin to keep him in sight and report his whereabouts, not "pursuing" with any intent to "confront."

"Putting together the timelines of the calls – hard evidence – and the testimony of the prosecution's 'star witness' Rachel Jeantel," Ayoob detailed.

Ayoob explained that when Zimmerman lost sight of Martin, the teen was not very far from his father's residence.

"Yet in the four minutes thereafter," Ayoob explained, "he (Martin) had to have left that location and gone toward Zimmerman's. Even Jeantel admits that the first words of the confrontation she heard were from Martin, before the phone went dead."

For more than two decades, Ayoob has been teaching the use of lethal force, and he understands the law. He noted that there is no law against watching somebody from a distance. However, it's not a good idea, in his opinion, to get out of a vehicle and go in foot pursuit of a suspicious person.

According to Ayoob, "Virtually all the evidence supports Zimmerman's account; no evidence contradicts it, and no evidence supports the theory that Zimmerman assaulted Martin first, in any way."

And Ayoob asks some pointed questions: "If as some conjecture Zimmerman had drawn the gun at the first, why did he wait until his scalp had been split open on the sidewalk and his nose smashed before he pulled the trigger? And if Martin really believed he was in danger from the man watching him, why didn't he simply call the police from the phone he was already speaking on?

"It's about evidence, not about 'what-ifs'," Ayoob explained, with some unkind remarks about how some in the press simply "twisted the facts" despite the lack of evidence to support any other theory about what happened. As he detailed the incident, there is but one conclusion, and that is "that Martin didn't like being watched, attacked Zimmerman violently, and was shot in self-defense by the man whose head he had been smashing against the sidewalk with potentially lethal effect."

Ayoob's full series is available on-line, and it should be considered "must reading" by anyone interested in the facts of the case, which ultimately lead to the truth, though in the 18 months leading up to the Zimmerman trial, and in the weeks following, truth often became as elusive as the Abominable Snowman, Sasquatch and the Loch Ness Monster.

Political theater

The press was very quick to portray Zimmerman as a police wannabe, a loser and racial profiler. These mischaracterizations, ultimately shown to be false, lingered throughout the investigation and trial, and among Zimmerman critics, still remain visceral.

Zimmerman's later misadventures in his personal life have nothing to do with the facts of the case; that single incident in a rainy neighborhood that would change his life forever, placing his every move, his every remark, under an unforgiving and some might even suggest blood thirsty media microscope. Every social misstep, every legal pratfall will be magnified and become national news, because in cases like Zimmerman's, hell hath no fury – or for that matter an unforgiving nature – like a disgruntled press.

The press can be a rather vindictive lot, and Zimmerman has hardly behaved as someone wishing to stay out of the media crosshairs. His treatment will be up to history to judge, so we will focus on that February 2012 incident and how it has been exploited and misrepresented.

Critics of Stand Your Ground (SYG) laws, which they have wrongfully claimed allow someone to get away with murder – an allegation that appears to have been made by even one juror in an interview with ABC News several days after the trial ended – only contributed to the public misunderstanding and racial animosity. There was some dispute that this interview created a false impression via careful editing, however. That juror in an unedited tape said the jury made the right decision based on the law, not on personal emotion. A writer for *Slate* suggested that the phrase "got away with murder" was part of the question that was asked, but not really part of the response. The longer version of the interview does not suggest this juror felt there was an error. She stood by the verdict, as *Slate* noted.

As it turned out at trial, the SYG law had nothing to do with the Zimmerman-Martin case. It was never brought up as part of the defense.

But in the political theater, everything is fair game, and exploitation of this case to further the agenda of anti-self-defense and anti-gun extremists became rampant.

Even Martin's mother, Sybrina Fulton, said that she was convinced the SYG law in Florida "played a role in her son's shooting death," according to the *Miami Herald*. She made that allegation while speaking to an audience in Miami Beach consisting of members of the National Bar Association, which has called for repeal of the law.

Lawmakers in liberal Connecticut got in on the act, announcing that they would "scrutinize their own state laws, including that concerning the use of deadly force in self-defense, for racial bias."

That's what was reported by the Connecticut Law Review, which noted that Connecticut's self-defense law varies considerably from the SYG statute in Florida. Democrat House Speaker Brendan Sharkey was quoted suggesting that because Zimmerman was a neighborhood watch volunteer, it might not be appropriate for him to carry a firearm. This ignored the fact that Zimmerman was not working as a watch captain that night, but was running errands, so why should he not be legally armed? None of the network talking heads asked that question because they would not like the answer.

Zimmerman was not even charged with a crime until many days after the incident, and it appears politics had a great deal to do with that. Florida Gov. Rick Scott appointed a special prosecutor and the second-degree murder charge was the result.

Initially, the police released Zimmerman after several hours of interrogation and for treatment of his head wounds. At the time, police investigating the case believed it was self-defense and that there was not enough evidence or legal grounds to make an arrest, which quickly became one of many demands from the African-American community fired up by the rhetoric of various high-profile civil rights scions, including Jesse Jackson and Al Sharpton.

But the appointment of Angela Corey as special prosecutor sent a clear signal that all bets and brakes were off. As Ayoob observed, "When Ms. Corey announced that she would bypass the grand jury, it was clear to any criminal justice professional that she was going to indict him on her own, via an offer of information. There is generally one reason why a chief prosecutor will take a case away from a grand jury: the prosecutor wants an indictment and doesn't think a grand jury that has heard the evidence will deliver one.

"At this point," Ayoob continued, "the die was cast. The show trial was inevitable, and America had experienced a triumph of propaganda that would have been worthy of Joseph Goebbels or Josef Stalin."

Now, more than two years after the incident and long after the trial has concluded, Ayoob acknowledged that most Americans are ignorant of the facts. Some might even suggest they are oblivious. Most of what remains in the public consciousness is the rhetoric, and the public – as he observed – seems "still convinced that a self-appointed vigilante racially profiled a black child and murdered him. Never mind that the facts in evidence clearly showed otherwise."

For those who practice the politics of emotion and race, it did not seem to matter that legal analysts were cautioning that the charge was going to be virtually impossible to prove and that there was not enough evidence for substantiation. The "activists" had an issue, a cooperative press and a spotlight. They were not going to allow this opportunity to escape them. Again, recalling the words of Chicago Mayor and former White House Chief of Staff Rahm Emanuel, "never let a crisis go to waste."

What had started as a rather routine investigation quickly became a cause. Even the Wikipedia version of the events noted that there was "widespread, intense and contradictory media coverage and misleading reporting."

Possibly at or near the top of misleading information was the media's repeated – and many believe deliberate – use of a years-old image of Martin that left the public with the impression that Zimmerman had gunned down a 12-year-old black child. Zimmerman shot a 17-year-old physically fit, and somewhat taller, individual who attacked him from the dark and, while allegedly reaching for his legally-carried pistol, allegedly threatened to kill him. This was after he had apparently slammed Zimmerman's head against the cement hard enough to draw blood.

But the image tactic also repeatedly depicted an unshaven Zimmerman, creating the impression that the man who had gunned down that child was a rather unsavory type. When Ayoob discussed this obvious slanting of the news reports, here's how he described it:

"The story fed to the press would outrage anyone…and, predictably, it outraged everyone. The family provided a picture of Trayvon at age 12 or 13, which the media ran with the ugliest picture of Zimmerman they could find. The meme of a huge armed adult 'stalking' a 'helpless child' was born fully grown, to a Godzilla-like size. It loomed over America unopposed.

However, as the investigation would reveal, as reported by Ayoob, investigators and the State's Attorney's Office had determined that Zimmerman was attacked by the teen, and was brutally beaten once on the ground.

"But cops and good lawyers don't try their cases in the press," he wrote from years of experience as a reserve police officer, investigator and expert witness, "and no voice rose loud enough with the facts to drown out the roar of the fantasy."

Had there not been an immediate media frenzy, it is possible charges never would have been filed, but as Ayoob reminded his readers, we are not dealing with "what if," but "what was."

For months afterward, the gun prohibition lobby took up the cause of attacking self-defense laws, including specifically the SYG statute in Florida. They also went after concealed carry laws, because one issue that seems to create considerable angst in the anti-gun movement is the fact that millions of law-abiding citizens have carry permits or licenses, or actually carry their firearms openly in many jurisdictions. This is not merely upsetting to many anti-gunners, it is frightening, yet there is no evidence that people who openly carry firearms pose any kind of threat to public safety.

Where SYG laws exist, they appear to be on firm ground with lots of public support, and some in the firearms community suspect that one of the reasons for much of the drama is to discourage lawmakers in other states from adopting similar statutes.

But the *Miami Herald* noted that since Florida adopted SYG in 2005, the state's violent crime rate had declined, while justifiable homicides had increased. At the Miami Beach event featuring Sybrina Fulton, the president of the National Bar Association, John Page – who is African-American – insisted that the law has allowed a disproportionate number of blacks to be affected. He insisted that the law is not necessary because a plea of self-defense was all that Zimmerman's attorneys needed to secure his acquittal.

The acquittal did not exonerate Zimmerman in the eyes of Attorney General Eric Holder, who allowed a Justice Department investigation to continue to determine if Martin's civil rights were violated.

The political environment where the Left was concerned took on something of a mob mentality. Where they had originally been satisfied that Zimmerman was arrested and charged with a crime, when the jury brought back its verdict, they demanded "justice" for Martin, which translated to punishment regardless of the verdict.

When President Barack Obama got involved with his now-infamous reference to Martin as being what his own son would look like, if he had a son, and followed up with a post-verdict statement that Martin could have been him 25 years ago, many saw that as just another form of race hucksterism.

'No justice, No peace'

Following the not guilty verdict, any lingering suspicion that the Left and many in the minority community would be satisfied that the system worked quickly evaporated as demonstrations erupted in cities all over the country. Placards bearing the ominous message "No justice, No peace" started appearing at these demonstrations, and in the weeks that followed, incidents unfolded that, while isolated, indicated that there was more at work than just disappointment over the verdict.

Backlash against the verdict begat the "This is for Trayvon" type of hate crime, whether it was associated with a robbery or just an assault.

The "No justice, No peace" slogan bears with it a subtle, and rather ugly threat. If the mob mentality doesn't get its way, there will be trouble, perhaps even violence. One cannot possibly tie the "This is for Trayvon" attacks to the broader movement of disappointment over the Zimmerman trial outcome. Such incidents are typically just the work of thugs looking for an excuse to commit a violent hate crime coupled with robbery.

But parading the threat of "no peace" unless Zimmerman were somehow punished provides all the motivation for a criminal element to take out their false revenge on other people.

Always just under the surface of these troubling stories was the campaign to erode gun rights and self-defense statutes so that people would either be discouraged from buying and owning firearms, and carrying them for personal protection, or the laws would be restrictively altered so as to make lawful self-defense a crime. Couple that with the veiled suggestion that the mere act of having a firearm or buying one for personal safety carried with it some kind of racist underpinning, and one has what at least some anti-gunners hoped was the recipe for an erosion of self-defense as a principle.

There is a significant problem with this strategy, of course. Bad people continue committing crimes and hurting good people in the process, and that does not go without notice. Social conscience gives way to self-preservation pretty fast, especially as more information surfaces about the facts surrounding the case.

But even with all of that, the press and a certain segment of the public continue to dwell on the case as a monumental injustice. They wanted Zimmerman convicted and punished. When the Florida court wouldn't do it, the media took over to demonize him.

The media lynch mob appears to have had very high hopes, and they were not prepared for the disappointment that came with the verdict.

Take the editorial that was published by the Buffalo, N.Y. *News* more than two weeks after the verdict. It dredged up the liberal disdain for SYG, asserting, "Trayvon Martin was killed and his shooter went free, in part because of the atrocity known as 'stand your ground' laws." In addition to comparing SYG to a war crime, the editorial said it was a "misbegotten law."

The editorial went on to quote former Broward County prosecutor David Frankel, who had been interviewed by the *Sun-Sentinal* newspaper in connection to a different SYG case in Florida: "It is an abomination. The ultimate intent might be good, but in practice, people take the opportunity to shoot first and say later they had a justification. It almost gives them a free pass to shoot."

The Zimmerman indictment and prosecution failed so indict the law and get it repealed; that quickly emerged as the strategy for press anti-gunners. They desperately needed some kind of "victory" (make that a punishment for all law-abiding citizens by removing a cornerstone of self-defense) to justify all the moral outrage they had created.

When President Obama involved himself in the debate, he made a remark for which he was lucky nobody in the White House press corps called him out.

"I'd just ask people to consider, if Trayvon Martin was of age and armed, could he have stood his ground on that sidewalk? And do we actually think that he would have been justified in shooting Mr. Zimmerman, who had followed him in a car, because he felt threatened? And if the answer to that question is at least ambiguous, then it seems to me that we might want to examine those kinds of laws."

The president was playing the race card and he knew it. Fortunately for him, nobody threw in the Joker. That was the case of Roderick Scott of Greece, N.Y. In April 2009, Scott – an African-American – was acquitted by a jury in the slaying of a white teen, Christopher Cervini, 16, who was confronted by Scott during what appeared to be break-ins of cars belonging to Scott's neighbors.

Cervini was almost the same age as Martin. He was described by his family as a "gentle child" who was "slaughtered."

According to a published report in Rochester, Scott confronted Cervini and two others and ordered them to "freeze" and wait for police to arrive. The teen allegedly charged at Scott, who shot him.

While there were parallels between the Zimmerman and Scott cases, there is one gaping disparity: Neither the president nor his attorney general weighed in on the case, nor were there expressions of outrage, no marches or other demonstrations, no wall-to-wall nightly news coverage, no Justice Department probe.

Instead there was peace because there had been justice.

No ability to retreat

SYG laws are known as such but in Washington State, where the principle is enshrined in court rulings rather than a statute, the principle is "no duty to retreat." Essentially, it boils down to a question of semantics, but as former *Washington Times* Senior Opinion Editor Emily Miller noted, Zimmerman could not have retreated from Martin's attack.

"There is no way that Mr. Zimmerman could have retreated because Mr. Martin was on top of him and beating him up on the ground," Miller wrote. "As the jury decided, Mr. Zimmerman was trapped and thought his life was in danger, so he was within his right to use lethal force to avoid being killed."

She accused the president of "milking" Martin's death "for all he can – first to stir up racial division and now to get more gun-control laws."

Miller pointed out another aspect of the case that was routinely – some suggest deliberately – ignored by the mainstream press and the left-leaning cable news networks. Zimmerman was knocked to the ground by the first blow from Martin. From that moment forward, it was physically impossible for him to retreat. He had nowhere to go because Martin was straddling him.

"The president also questioned whether these state laws 'are designed in such a way that they may encourage the kinds of altercations and confrontations and tragedies that we saw in the Florida case, rather than defuse potential altercations, if there's a way for them to exit from a situation'," Miller noted.

In that, Mr. Obama inserted his foot in mouth again obviously without intent, because had he thought his comment through, it would have been clear he was refuting his own argument. Zimmerman had no way to exit from the situation in which he found himself. The laws are hardly designed to enable people to engage in a confrontation, and the president knew it. Any self-defense authority would tell the president that one essentially loses a self-defense argument if it can be shown that he voluntarily engaged in any altercation that escalated to the point where he had to use lethal forced to extract himself. The laws do not work that way.

As Ayoob noted earlier in this chapter, the evidence shows that Zimmerman was responding to the police dispatcher's caution that it was not necessary for him to follow Martin. It was after breaking off that endeavor that the confrontation occurred.

One other thing that many people contended was that the only crime apparently committed that night was a criminal assault by Trayvon Martin, when he struck George Zimmerman. Prior to that, nothing illegal had happened.

However, once again, critics of the verdict who were not prepared to see Zimmerman acquitted stubbornly still cling to the fallacy that there was no justice in the jury's decision. They essentially "wanted blood," a pound of flesh, an eye for an eye, and when they didn't get it, their fury and failed expectations got the better of them, or perhaps their pre-existing prejudices simply surfaced.

Years ago, author Walter Van Tilburg Clark wrote a novel about a lynching called *The Oxbow Incident*. It was made into a classic western by William Wellman, and starred Henry Fonda, Dana Andrews, Harry Morgan and several other great character actors. It was the story of a posse that turned into a kill-crazed lynch mob that set upon three drifters they suspected of being involved in a murder and cattle rustling.

After some deliberation, albeit not much, the posse – without benefit of a trial – hanged the three only to later learn no murder had actually occurred, that the victim had survived and identified his attackers, and that the posse had lynched the wrong men. It is a powerful story about people acting on cursory and erroneous information to deadly effect.

The mainstream press could never be indicted as a whole for inciting a mob, but reporting about Zimmerman in the days after the shooting is reminiscent of Richard Jewell, the man who tried to warn authorities about a suspicious backpack at the Atlanta Olympics in 1996. The bomb exploded and in the aftermath, Jewell was implicated as a suspect by the FBI, only to be exonerated a couple of months later. He was never charged with a crime. By then, however, the damage to his reputation was done and he filed libel lawsuits against news agencies for their reporting.

Mr. Jewell died in 2007, but he will always be remembered as the man connected to the Atlanta bombing, but at least he did see his name cleared.

CHAPTER 8

BEING STUPID IN PUBLIC LETS EVERYONE KNOW

People in the gun prohibition movement can be monumentally stupid with their remarks or actions, as noted in Chapter Three's discussions regarding Colorado's Diana DeGette and Vice President Joe Biden, and their chief problem – and one that invariably affects their credibility – is that they say and do these things in public.

Whether they are being insulting to a crime victim in Colorado or talking gun control on some television program, writing something foolish or speaking from a Congressional or legislative podium, there are simply incidents that you could not make up if you wanted to. They capture the essence of people who pontificate on subjects about which they have absolutely no knowledge, only an opinion that is more often than not grounded in myth and utter nonsense.

If any of these people were to read the gun control playbook from cover to cover, they would at least understand why they are counseled to keep their arguments on an emotional level. It is because they are "factually challenged" when it comes to actual data or real-life experience.

This is not to say some individuals in the gun rights movement do not have their own moments of ineptitude – such as the people who attribute quotes to George Washington or Adolph Hitler that no historical research has ever been able to confirm. But when it comes to looking the fool, especially where firearms are concerned, gun prohibitionists definitely hold the low ground.

Writing for *Outdoor Life*, author John Haughey assembled a list of "dumbest gun-control quotes from politicians and celebrities" that included Biden's foolishness about home defense with a double-barreled shotgun, and a few other gems. Among them was actor Danny Glover's incredulous assertion that "The Second Amendment comes from the right to protect themselves from slave revolts, and from uprisings by Native Americans. A revolt from people who were stolen from their land or revolt from people whose land was stolen from, that's what the genesis of the Second Amendment is."

Glover is not the only person to make this argument, and it represents what one might consider to be a tortured twisting of history to fit one's political narrative. Long story short, it carries the subliminal suggestion that supporting the Second Amendment has some kind of racist underpinning, same as being in favor of self-defense and "Stand Your Ground" laws.

The argument was picked up by Congressman Hank Johnson, the Georgia Democrat who invariably speaks in a condescending tone that suggests he is trying to sound like a great orator by dramatically drawing out his every word. According to Haughey's analysis, it is Johnson's position that the National Rifle Association does not support President Barack Obama because the NRA is a racist organization.

That might be difficult to explain to the countless minorities who are NRA members, including several prominent African-American gun owners.

Johnson will be forever remembered as the congressman who once asked Admiral Robert Willard – then commander of the U.S. Pacific fleet – if a planned military buildup on the island of Guam might cause a disaster one can only imagine in an old Warner Brothers cartoon.

"My fear," Johnson declared to the amused astonishment of everyone else in the room, "is that the whole island will become so overly populated that it will tip over and capsize."

Adm. Willard, in a classic upper echelon exercise of self-control (though he did show a bit of a grin) replied to the congressman, "We don't anticipate that."

Later, Johnson insisted he had merely been joking but if so, he had a lot of people fooled. He subsequently released a statement, quoted by CBS News, in which he said, "The subtle humor of this obviously metaphorical reference to a ship capsizing illustrated my concern about the impact of the planned military buildup on this small tropical island."

Anti-gun California Sen. Dianne Feinstein raised more than a few eyebrows when she was debating a ban on so-called "assault weapons" and full capacity magazines. She told her colleagues that, "We have federal regulations and state laws that prohibit hunting ducks with more than three rounds. And yet it's legal to hunt humans with 15-round, 30-round, even 150-round magazines."

Feinstein may want to consult with state fish and game agencies about that, not to mention state and local police agencies. The veteran gun prohibitionist, who once admitted that if she had had the votes at one point, she would have banned guns and told Americans to turn them in, seemed to suggest that it is now legal to "hunt people."

One might reasonably ask, "What kind of person comes up with that kind of observation?" That's not a sarcastic question, it is serious. What goes on in the mind of someone who suggests that it is legal to hunt people with a firearm? If that doesn't concern you, it should, especially if that individual is a United States Senator.

Haughey turned his attention to New York Congresswoman Louise Slaughter, another anti-gun Democrat who, according to his account, made the preposterous assertion that many people buy semiautomatic sport utility rifles because they want to engage in a battle with the federal government.

"The idea of fighting the government with an AR-15, and I know that's an idea a lot of people have; if they ever look, as I have, at what the federal defense budget is, I think they would disabuse themselves of that notion right away," Slaughter said during a television interview.

Haughey skipped Congresswoman Sheila Jackson Lee of Texas, whose career is astonishing because she continues getting elected. In the spring of 2013 as she was promoting an anti-gun bill on the House floor, Jackson Lee blamed guns, not inner city gangsters, for a wave of violence on the streets.

"Don't condemn the gangbangers," she said (with a straight face), "they've got guns that are trafficked, that are not enforced, that are straw purchased and they come into places even that have strong gun laws. Why? Because we don't have sensible gun legislation."

Wait just one minute. The gun laws now on the books that prohibit gun trafficking and straw purchasing were all pandered as "sensible" when they were propelled through Congress.

Jackson Lee's defense of gangbangers as some kind of victim of trafficked guns might easily be called "mind numbingly stupid."

Then there is vehemently anti-gun Congresswoman Carolyn McCarthy, whose family was touched by the violent Long Island commuter train shooting, and she ran for Congress on a gun control platform. But she has become an example of what is wrong with gun prohibitionists who have no clue about what they are trying to accomplish.

Back in 2007, when she was pushing for a ban on so-called "assault weapons," McCarthy was caught in an embarrassing moment when she was discussing certain characteristics and cosmetics of the guns she wanted banned, a reporter asked her about barrel shrouds. (The shroud is part of the forend that covers a rifle barrel to prevent a shooter from burning his or her hand when the barrel is hot.)

"I actually don't know what a barrel shroud is," McCarthy admitted. "I believe it's a shoulder thing that goes up."

One needn't look too far in the political arena to find an anti-gun pol who has said something remarkably foolish. Marion Berry, former mayor of Washington, D.C. who became a convicted felon and then was re-elected to the city council, imparted this sage observation – quoted in *USA Today* – that, "Outside of the killings, D.C. has one of the lowest crime rates in the country."

Liberal anti-gun Congressman John Conyers of Michigan perhaps explained the mentality of the Far Left best when it comes to dealing with any legislation they want passed, no matter what. In this case it was Obamacare, but he could easily have been talking about any number of gun control measures he has supported over the years.

"I love these members, they get up and say, 'Read the bill'... What good is reading the bill if it's a thousand pages and you don't have two days and two lawyers to find out what it means after you read the bill?"

State senators blow it

Two state senators in Washington became laughingstocks when a measure they co-sponsored in 2013 to ban so-called "assault weapons" was unceremoniously revealed to contain a provision for unannounced, warrantless annual searches of private homes by sheriff's deputies in order to see that gun owners were in compliance with storage requirements of the proposed legislation.

One of the two, perennially anti-gun Sen. Adam Kline, was caught in something of a fib when he insisted that he did not realize the provision was in his bill. That blew up in his face within days when it was discovered that two previous gun ban bills introduced by him during past legislative sessions contained the same provision.

Worse still was the "Nancy Pelosi moment" Kline and fellow sponsor Ed Murray – both represented legislative districts in Seattle – admitted that they had not actually read the legislation they were sponsoring. It turned out that the bill had been something of a "cut and paste" product using language from a gun control organization's "model" as the basis for the bill.

A pro-gun control *Seattle Times* columnist, Danny Westneat, zeroed in on the story but tried to provide the two liberal Democrat lawmakers with a bit of cover by insisting, "That lawmakers sponsor bills they haven't read is common. Still, it's disappointing on one of this political magnitude."

That bit of excuse-making did not register with angry Washington gun owners. They furiously flooded Olympia with telephone calls and e-mails and the legislation died almost immediately.

Still in Washington, when former Seattle Mayor Mike McGinn and Washington Ceasefire Board President Ralph Fascitelli launched a discriminatory program that encouraged businesses to declare their premises "gun free zones," Fascitelli admitted that the effort would not prevent a violent criminal from carrying out an attack.

"We know this won't stop someone determined to cause violence," he acknowledged, "but we hope that standing together and giving businesses a tool to say no to guns will change the conversation around gun violence. Maybe our message will even make it to Olympia – we need better tools now to stop gun violence in our community."

Even reporters covering the story at the time marveled at this, wondering privately why, if something is admittedly not going to have an effect, anyone would want to do it.

The answer is that each one of these efforts amounts to a trophy if it scores even modest success, and brings contributions through the door. It keeps them "relevant" at a time when their relevancy was questionable. It gets them publicity. The fact that more than two dozen Seattle businesses – restaurants, coffee shops and small retail stores and bars – signed on to this program of wishful thinking was a "big deal" to McGinn in particular because he could use it as a campaign issue in his effort to get re-elected.

This and similar projects around the country are symbolic gestures and nothing more, despite claims to the contrary. They do not prevent crimes, and there is ample evidence they may even contribute to the effectiveness of mass shootings because none of the intended victims is able to fight back.

It amounts to what Fascitelli said about the Seattle effort: "We're making a statement as a community."

That's wonderful, so long as one understands that criminals and madmen looking for a headline will not be listening to any statement, and even if they did, they would pay no attention.

Such efforts provide a false and some might say delusional sense of safety, right up to the moment another horrible crime unfolds.

Another politician in a different state – Rep. Joe Salazar, a Colorado Democrat – inserted his foot into his mouth during a controversial debate on gun control measures in that state early in 2013. Explaining his opposition to allowing legally-carried firearms on college campuses, especially by women concerned about sexual assault, Salazar had this to say:

"It's why we have call boxes, it's why we have safe zones, it's why we have the whistles. Because you just don't know who you're gonna be shooting at. And you don't know if you feel like you're gonna be raped, or if you feel like someone's been following you around or if you feel like you're in trouble when you may actually not be, that you pop out that gun and you pop … pop a round at somebody."

He admitted that "there are some gender inequities on college campuses."

Salazar subsequently offered an apology for having offended anyone with his remarks, but he did not explain whether a "safe zone" is actually that at all, or just a "zone of happy thoughts" as one attorney put it after having to explain what is wrong with so-called "gun free zones."

Stick to singing

Aging crooner Tony Bennett probably should stick to music, because his entry into the gun control arena was simply astonishing. Bennett, who was 86 at the time, was commenting on the right to keep and bear arms, and so-called "gun violence" in the wake of the Sandy Hook tragedy.

"It's the kind of turn that happened to the great country of Germany," Bennett said, "when Nazis came over and created tragic things, and they had to be told off. And if we continue this kind of violence and accept it in our country, the rest of the world's going to really take care of us, in a very bad way."

If you found yourself wondering what Bennett was talking about, do not be dismayed. It didn't make a lot of sense to anyone else.

Of course, Mr. Bennett is hardly the only entertainer who has said something foolish about guns in public. Rosie O'Donnell would be at or near the front of the line when it comes to handing out awards for putting one's foot in one's mouth when discussing firearms.

During the heyday of her television talk show, Ms. O'Donnell famously insisted that, "I don't care if you want to hunt, I don't care if you think it's your right. I say 'Sorry.' We have had enough as a nation. You are not allowed to own a gun, and if you do own a gun I think you should go to prison.'"

O'Donnell's infamous ambush of actor Tom Selleck in May 1999, who at the time was featured in a National Rifle Association advertisement, blew up in her face with many viewers who were more admiring of Selleck than the talk host.

Years later, she admitted that she was "pretty raw." According to one account, she admitted to having been on antidepressants and had not slept much after the April 1999 massacre at Columbine High School in Littleton, Colorado.

O'Donnell repeatedly called Selleck a spokesman for the NRA, which he repeatedly denied.

At one point she told Selleck that she believed the Second Amendment was in the constitution "so we could have muskets when the British people come over in 1800."

In the *New York Post* article about that outburst, which ran for more than seven minutes, O'Donnell said she was "overwhelmingly distraught in a manner that, my therapist said, was not specifically germane to the issue."

Well, that explains everything.

Then again, perhaps it doesn't. Ms. O'Donnell had to acknowledge that – despite her abhorrence toward private firearms ownership – she employed an armed bodyguard, but insisted it was for her children.

That sounded suspiciously like something singer James Taylor said during a January 2013 interview with *The Daily Caller*. Acknowledging that the nation "is very divided on gun control," he told the publication that, "I think the majority of us feel strongly — even the majority of gun owners feel strongly — that we need to make some sacrifice[s] to our freedoms, if that's the way to put it. We need to make some sacrifices to what we might want to have, in order to safeguard our children."

That might come as a surprise to gun owners who have no intention of sacrificing any of their freedom, or their firearms. Indeed, the firearms fraternity would tell Mr. Taylor that it's the very possession of firearms that keeps their families, and especially their children, safe.

Actor Jason Alexander, best known for his part in the Jerry Seinfeld sitcom, wrote down his thoughts following the Sandy Hook tragedy and came across as a loony extremist.

"There is no excuse for the propagation of these weapons," he said about so-called "assault rifles" like the one used by killer Adam Lanza. "They are not guaranteed or protected by our constitution. If they were, then we could all run out and purchase a tank, a grenade launcher, a bazooka, a SCUD missile and a nuclear warhead. We could stockpile napalm and chemical weapons and bomb-making materials in our cellars under our guise of being a militia."

Reality explained

Perhaps nobody has explained the reality of the situation better than commentator Thomas Sowell in The American Spectator, in an article headlined, "Invincible Ignorance." Just days after the Sandy Hook tragedy when the country was being overwhelmed by a hysteria-motivated discussion about the need for tougher gun laws, Sowell took a more realistic approach.

"Must every tragic mass shooting bring out the shrill ignorance of 'gun control' advocates," he inquired. "The key fallacy of so-called gun control laws is that such laws do not in fact control guns. They simply disarm law-abiding citizens, while people bent on violence find firearms readily available."

This is what gun rights activists have been contending for years. Sowell challenged "gun control zealots" for having no "respect for facts." He noted that jurisdictions with the toughest gun laws have often had the highest murder rates.

But Sowell didn't stop there. Noting that the rate of gun ownership is higher in rural America than in urban centers, he also pointed out that the murder rate is higher in the cities. And then Sowell, an African-American, dropped a couple of bombs.

"The rate of gun ownership is higher among whites than among blacks," Sowell continued, "but the murder rate is higher among blacks. For the country as a whole, handgun ownership doubled in the late 20th century, while the murder rate went down."

Many self-styled "progressives" would look at that statement and try to twist the argument into something about race simply because Sowell stated a very uncomfortable fact having to do with the disturbingly high murder rate in black communities, such as Chicago, New Orleans and Washington, D.C.

But the political left does not wish to deal with this, or even face it. Apologists invariably try to spin the debate so it solely focuses on guns rather than the broader issue of violent and vulgar rap music, the "gangsta" lifestyle that attracts far too many inner city minorities, and the breakdown of the family structure – or simply the lack of one – in the minority community.

One could argue that is what liberal Daily Beast columnist and Fox News contributor Kirsten Powers did during a debate over the slaying of Australian baseball player Christopher Lane in August 2013 by three youths in an Oklahoma town. The trio, according to initial reports, killed the visiting athlete because they were bored.

When Powers debated this case on the popular O'Reilly Factor with Republican strategist Kate Obenshain, she deflected away from the issue of violent music and other entertainment and went right for the low-hanging fruit of any debate about violent crime in America.

She blamed the "gun culture" for the killing.

"Our gun culture…is what is behind this," she insisted.

Obenshain countered, "It's not about gun culture this is about a culture of violence that is promoted among our young people. It is imperative that we have this discussion. This issue will be swept under the rug by people who just want to talk about guns."

Powers might be just the person to explain the irony of what happened in Boulder County, Colorado in the wake of the state's adoption of new gun control laws, the organizers of a gun buyback had to cancel the event. According to the Associated Press, Boulder County Sheriff Joe Pelle said the news laws would make it almost impossible to conduct the buyback because it would be tough for everybody to comply.

The group would have had to retain the services of a licensed firearms dealer. Transfers of firearms would have required background checks, for which the retailer would have had to be paid. Gun prohibitionists who tried to stage the event were "disappointed." But now they at least had gotten a taste of what they pushed onto the shoulders of gun owners.

Back to school

Writing in opposition to the notion that armed security or even armed teachers in public schools could prevent or at least bring to an end another lethal school attack like Columbine or Sandy Hook, writers almost seem obliged to suggest the real danger is a student getting hold of the gun, or a teacher pulling a gun on a student.

Rocco Pendola, writing on The Street, opposed a move to arm teachers at a Clarksville, Arkansas school. He wondered how long it might be before "a teacher feels 'threatened' by a student and pulls the gun on the pupil just to defuse the perceived threat. Or the school employee cannot restrain him or herself and blows the kid's brains out in front of a classroom full of terrified children. Or maybe, in self-defense, students wrestle a firearm away from the teacher who pulled it. Or there's a meeting between school officials and the parents of a child receiving disciplinary action. Disagreement ensues. Things get intense. A packing assistant principal pulls out her heat."

These are loaded arguments, no pun intended, and they are designed to reach readers on an emotional level rather than a factual one supported by any data that such things have happened.

Pendola subsequently acknowledged what might best be described as a contradiction of logic.

"Now let me be clear," he wrote. "I am not one of these ardent anti-gun cats. If I had my choice, I would prefer fewer guns, not proliferation into my child's school. But, on the issue of guns in general, I don't have a strong opinion one way or the other."

However, he then acknowledged, "Before last November, the closest I ever came to a gun was when I got pulled over by a police officer. The things have always terrified me."

One might suggest that being "terrified" of a firearm indicates a pretty "strong opinion" about guns.

Jakob Reynolds, writing as a columnist for the *Daily Toreador* at Texas Tech, also contended that guns on a school campus are bad.

"There are numerous flaws with such policy," Reynolds wrote. "Unless schools that arm teachers also are willing to pay for and write in basic firearm safety education to their curricula, introducing guns to a classroom setting increases the chances that a firearm will end up in the untrained hands of a student."

It's essentially the same argument with a slight twist, but it suggests an unfounded fear, or a crafted anti-gun straw man argument, that a defensive firearm will almost invariably end up in the wrong hands. As such, it is not much of an argument.

Evidently that is what many school districts think as well, because when the 2013-14 school year began in many areas, there were armed teachers or armed security personnel on campus. It was a remarkable reversal of the mantra of but a few months earlier in the wake of the Sandy Hook tragedy, with the adoption of a philosophy initially put forth by the National Rifle Association.

Newspapers were fairly balanced in reporting the introduction of armed security at schools because it seemed to be a "local" idea when the press had earlier demonized the NRA approach as an "extremist" reaction, which smacked of hypocrisy.

NRA Executive Vice President Wayne LaPierre famously – or infamously, depending upon one's philosophy – told a press conference that "The only thing that stops a bad guy with a gun is a good guy with a gun."

But college writer Reynolds in the *Daily Toreador* lamented, "Even if bringing guns into the classroom makes the few teachers who genuinely want to carry handguns in the classroom feel in some way empowered, it puts additional stress on other teachers and students as a whole and detracts from the open learning environment the public school classroom is supposed to be.

"Many of my peers in the Texas public education system and I who went through primary and secondary education were taught various methods and reasons to sort out our differences through non-violent means," he wrote.

He seems to compare a schoolyard argument with a classroom full of students being attacked by a madman with a firearm. Reynolds may not understand this, but those "various methods and reasons to sort out… differences" are not going to be very effective when someone is preparing to shoot at you, or has already opened fire.

Lastly, Reynolds pulled something of a disingenuous sleight of hand when he commented, "Another aspect of arming teachers that its proponents seem to miss is the fact that armed civilians have stopped very few mass shootings. A study conducted by *Mother Jones* found that in the past 30 years, there have been 62 mass shootings — defined by the FBI as occurring in a public place and having four or more fatalities — of which only two were stopped by armed civilians, and of whom one was gravely injured and the other shot and killed."

That sounds impressive until one realizes that virtually all mass shootings have occurred in so-called "gun free zones" where even law-abiding citizens are unilaterally disarmed by laws, regulations or private property paranoia. Of course armed citizens haven't stopped such incidents because there were no armed citizens present to take action.

Perhaps Reynolds, or someone from *Mother Jones*, might like to try a mass shooting at a gun range or gun store. That might provide conclusive evidence whether someone is mistaken about the response capability and effectiveness of an armed citizen in the middle of mayhem.

CHAPTER 9

MEET THE BIGGEST LIARS OF THEM ALL

George Orwell, author of *Nineteen Eighty-Four*, and Joseph Goebbels, chief Nazi propagandist for Adolph Hitler, both understood the psychology of "The Big Lie."

Novelist Orwell chillingly portrayed this phenomenon in its worst possible light while Goebbels hideously turned it into an art form.

Orwell perhaps put it best when he expounded on a key element of the totalitarian society that led people "to tell deliberate lies while genuinely believing in them, to forget any fact that has become inconvenient, and then, when it becomes necessary again, to draw it back from oblivion for just as long as it is needed, to deny the existence of objective reality and all the while to take account of the reality which one denies – all this is indispensably necessary."

Goebbels, on the other hand, was a bit more direct: "Propaganda should be popular, not intellectually pleasing. It is not the task of propaganda to discover intellectual truths."

Orwell tried to warn us about the abuses that come with spinning falsehoods so they become fact. Goebbels was the chief practitioner, the fellow who essentially perfected turning lies into truths. Let us examine one small example of how something that is demonstrably false is so oft-repeated that it essentially becomes an accepted "fact."

The gun control playbook contends that "A critical flaw in the background check system is the loophole that results in two out of every five guns sold in America changing hands without a background check."

One month after the Sandy Hook tragedy in Newtown, Connecticut, President Barack Obama asserted, "The law already requires licensed gun dealers to run background checks, and over the last 14 years that's kept 1.5 million of the wrong people from getting their hands on a gun. But it's hard to enforce that law when as many as 40 percent of all gun purchases are conducted without a background check."

108

This 40 percent figure is repeated in his plan for "reducing gun violence" in American communities, and Vice President Joe Biden, addressing the U.S. Conference of Mayors, insisted, "Studies show that up to 40 percent of the people — and there's no — let me be honest with you again, which I'll get to in a moment. Because of the lack of the ability of federal agencies to be able to even keep records, we can't say with absolute certainty what I'm about to say is correct. But the consensus is about 40 percent of the people who buy guns today do so outside the NICS (National Instant Criminal Background Check) system, outside the background check system."

But no less than the *Washington Post*, among the leading liberal cheerleaders for gun control, reported about a week after those statements were made, in an article headlined "The stale claim that 40 percent of gun sales lack background checks," that the study from which that 40-percent figure was taken was based on data that was nearly 20 years old. Most importantly, the data came from a period before and just after the Brady background check law was passed, and before that law was fully implemented.

After careful review with one of the researchers responsible for the 1997 Institute of Justice report from whence the figure was pulled, the *Washington Post* Fact Checker column essentially "called bullshit" on the claim, giving the contention a devastating "four Pinocchio" rating, essentially classifying it as a bald-faced lie.

What is disturbing about this is that the 40 percent figure has been repeatedly used even after the newspaper revealed the credibility problem. It is one of those things that simply will not go away, as it has become part of the anti-gun dogma, much like the belief that gun shows are "arms bazaars for criminals and crazy people."

This idea is further ingrained in the gun control playbook's text: "We should emphasize the need to stop private sales from being a device where criminals, people with severe mental illness, and terrorists can easily acquire the most dangerous weapons. All we are asking is for all gun purchasers to be required to pass background checks that help keep guns out of the hands of criminals, terrorists and the seriously mentally ill."

It is not that the authors were aware their assertion is bogus, but more likely that they simply accepted and repeated it for the benefit of making their argument, without doing any research. The playbook was assembled prior to the *Washington Post's* revelations.

Still, this attack on gun shows as the source of firearms for criminals of all stripes does not hold water, again thanks to the *Washington Post* Fact

Checker. About one week prior to the publication of a book titled *Reducing Gun Violence in America*, by Daniel Webster, director of the Johns Hopkins Center for Gun Policy, the newspaper noted that Webster used data from a 2004 survey of state prison inmates who had used handguns.

According to the *Post*, "The offenders were incarcerated from crimes committed with handguns, and this is how they reported how they obtained the guns:

> Licensed gun dealer: 11 percent
> Friends or family: 39.5 percent
> "The street:" 37.5 percent
> Stolen gun: 9.9 percent
> Gun show/Flea market: 1.7 percent

That last figure is important, because it has been consistent for several years. Yet, in their repeated efforts to close this so-called "gun show loophole," the gun prohibition lobby continually insists that this is critical to keeping guns out of the wrong hands. This simply defies logic for anyone familiar with the data, but it appears that anti-gunners believe – correctly, perhaps – that the majority of people are not aware of the data and simply accept the "loophole" demon as being quite genuine.

Indeed, when it comes to perpetuating a falsehood, Goebbels and the villains in *Nineteen Eighty-Four* had nothing on today's gun prohibitionists.

And the term "loophole" is generously, if not carelessly, applied to virtually anything with which gun prohibitionists disagree. The word has become something of a sneering epithet, causing some in the gun rights community to suggest that "the Second Amendment is a loophole for these people."

Dancing in Fake Blood

Samuel Clemens, aka Mark Twain, once remarked that there are "Lies, Damned Lies and Statistics," and when it comes to the gun prohibition lobby, they engage in the first two using – or should we say mis-using – data to inflate the number of people they claim are victims of "gun violence."

We'll put it another way. The only people who enjoy dancing in blood more than anti-gunners are vampires.

In the promotional statement for *Reducing Gun Violence in America* on *Amazon.com*, the first line observes, "The staggering toll of gun violence—which claims 31,000 U.S. lives each year—is an urgent public health issue that demands an effective evidence-based policy response."

Likewise, when Washington Ceasefire President Ralph Fascitelli appeared at a media event in Seattle, touting a program that convinced local businesses to declare themselves "gun free zones," he told reporters in the room that "Gun violence has become an epidemic in our country, claiming more than 31,000 lives every year."

But is that accurate? Are these actual homicide victims? Do that many people die annually as murder victims? Is there really an "epidemic" of gun violence?

Absolutely not, and anti-gunners know it. We discussed this data deception briefly in Chapter 6.

Consistently over the past few years, the Federal Bureau of Investigation's annual crime report says somewhere in the neighborhood of 12,000 to 13,000 people are actually murdered every year, and of those, between 8,000 and 9,000 are killed with some type of firearm.

Where do those other "victims of gun violence" come from, then? We've explained this: The 31,000 figure is a combination of murders, suicides and accidents.

The U.S. Department of Justice estimates that 60 percent of all adult firearms-related deaths are suicides. There is considerable debate about defining suicides as victims of "gun violence," same as people who are accidentally shot, such as in hunting or target shooting mishaps, or accidents in the home.

Likewise, this number would include all of those people killed justifiably by police or armed private citizens in self-defense. Those individuals aren't murder victims, either.

But it is far more dramatic to inflate the body count to a much larger all-encompassing figure because this creates the deliberately false impression that more than 30,000 persons are murdered every year, which simply is not the case. It is dishonest manipulation of data, and public perception.

That can also be said about Michael Bloomberg's "Everytown for Gun Safety" campaign, mentioned in Chapter One. Following a June 2014 school shooting in Troutdale, Oregon – also mentioned in Chapter One – the "Everytown" group was quoted by CNN, asserting that there had been 74 school shootings in the 18 months between the Sandy Hook tragedy and the Troutdale incident.

Incredibly, CNN reported that figure without first checking its veracity. It was only a day later, after a curious journalist named Charles Johnson debunked the figure by showing that the majority of those alleged "school shootings" had nothing to do with schools, other than proximity, that CNN did the responsible thing and checked.

"The statistic came from a group called Everytown for Gun Safety, an umbrella group started by former New York Mayor Michael Bloomberg, a passionate and public advocate of gun control," CNN was obliged to acknowledge.

Trying to couch its use of an unverified statistic, from an obviously biased source, CNN stressed, "Everytown says on its web site that it gleans its information from media reports and that its list includes school shootings involving a firearm discharged inside or on school grounds, including assaults, homicides, suicides and accidental shootings.

"CNN determined that 15 of the incidents Everytown included were situations similar to the violence in Oregon – a minor or adult actively shooting inside or near a school," the network explained. "That works out to about one shooting every five weeks."

Of course, 15 shootings is 15 too many, but that doesn't forgive CNN for its sloppiness. You can rest assured that CNN, or any other network in the left-leaning so-called "mainstream" media would meticulously scrutinize any data it received from the NRA, SAF, CCRKBA or any other gun rights organization.

Disclosure that the "74 shootings" figure was bogus did not stop the gun prohibition lobby from using it. Shannon Watts, founder of the Bloomberg-financed Moms Demand Action for Gun Sense in America (MDA) bylined an article that was published by the *New York Daily News* in which she stated, "(T)hese shootings also reinforce a troubling reality: 74 school shootings have occurred in the last 18 months since the massacre at Sandy Hook Elementary, yet elected officials have continually failed to enact common-sense reforms to fix our broken gun laws."

That "Everytown" and MDA are both financed by Bloomberg should make any information they release suspect. This episode proved it.

Sometimes, an anti-gunner simply isn't very careful with their use of words, or perhaps this is deliberate.

Writing on *PolicyMic* in December 2012, author Russ Cane stated, "In the United States, the total number of hand gun (sic) deaths (1980-2006) is more than 32,000 per year." This passage appears to misquote the source, a report from the Firearm and Injury Prevention Center, which noted, "In the last twenty-four years, an average of 32,300 Americans died each year from firearm injuries."

That figure represents fatalities involving all kinds of firearms, including handguns, rifles and shotguns. The FBI Uniform Crime Report breaks it down to weapon types, so this is not difficult to figure out. Recall that we discussed some of these figures in Chapter Six, and how the gun prohibition lobby inflates its numbers.

In 2012, the most recent year for which data was available at this writing, the FBI reported 12,765 murders, of which 8,855 were committed with firearms. Of those, 6,371 involved handguns. Another 322 were committed with rifles and 303 with shotguns. There were 1,859 involving firearms that were not described.

Then come other weapons. Knives or other cutting instruments accounted for 1,589 slayings, blunt objects were used on 518 people and "personal weapons" (hands, feet) killed 674 people.

The figure 12,765 is a far cry from 32,000, and 8,855 is even farther, about 73 percent of the total real homicide figure if one does a breakdown. Again, it is more dramatic to have the American public believe that there are more than 30,000 murders annually because it creates the impression that this country is awash in blood and guns, and one can argue that this is exactly why gun prohibitionists do it.

In the process, the gun control crowd perhaps realizes that the average American is not going to rush to the nearest laptop and log onto the FBI website to check their so-called facts. If citizens were to do that, they would quickly discover a loophole – dare we call it that? – in the "gun violence" narrative.

Over the course of five years, from 2008 through 2012, the number of homicides consistently declined. In 2008, according to the FBI's data, there were 14,224 homicides of which 9,528 were committed with firearms. In 2009, the number of murders topped out at 13,752 and 9,199 of those involved firearms. The following year, 2010 saw 13,164 homicides in which 8,874 involved firearms. In 2011, the homicide total dropped again to 12,795, with 8,653 of them being gun-related. We noted the 2012 statistics above.

Suicide is, of course, a horrible step for someone to take, though how does suicide with a firearm square with those who defend the "death with dignity" movement?

Let's let someone from the Death with Dignity National Center explain it. Melissa Barber, an electronic communications specialist with the Death with Dignity National Center said in an interview with *Caring.com*:

"The greatest human freedom is to live, and die, according to one's own desires and beliefs. From advance directives to physician-assisted dying, death with dignity is a movement to provide options for the dying to control their own end-of-life care."

"A key aspect of the Death with Dignity laws in Oregon and Washington is that patients must self-administer medication prescribed under the safeguards of the laws," she stated.

But that sounds like suicide, doesn't it? For advocates of Death with Dignity, it isn't. There are safeguards built into the laws, she explained. Those wishing to end their lives must go through "a lengthy request process" and they must be suffering from a terminal illness. People who are merely depressed or disappointed with life do not qualify. Terminally-ill patients self-administer the medications prescribed.

For gun prohibitionists, this may make all the difference.

A question that comes up frequently in the aftermath of a mass shooting, when the perpetrator commits suicide with the last shot fired, is "If this crazy person wanted to kill himself, why did he have to kill all of those innocent people first? Why not just crawl into a corner and do it without killing anybody else?"

Thanks in part to the media's fascination with that sort of crime, the social losers and crazy people who commit such acts just might wish to give themselves some immortality with a heinous act that gets headlines. Otherwise, these desperate loons would forever just be nobodies.

But there is something else. An assisted suicide – that is, a dignified death with the aid of some drug – is somehow cleaner than suicide with a firearm. Of course, it is nonsense to look at it that way because the individual is just as deceased. Only the method is different, yet anti-gunners constantly misrepresent suicide by firearm as gun violence, equating this final act with a homicide. At best that is disingenuous.

How does suicide by carbon monoxide (turn the car on in a closed garage), or hanging one's self differ from "assisted suicide/death with dignity?" How about jumping off a cliff or a building? Throwing one's self in front of a car, truck, bus or train? If we are comparing a "clean" form of suicide with a "messy" one, there is not much messier a method of suicide as leaping off a building or a cliff, or throwing one's self in front of an oncoming train or large motor vehicle.

And what about "suicide by cop?" This is known and identified method of self-imposed death that one might also call "assisted suicide." Commit a violent act or create the impression you are about to by aiming a gun at a police officer, and you're history.

These firearms-related deaths end up in the national statistics under the "homicide by gun" heading because people who are shot by police in a "suicide by cop" scenario are legally classified as "homicides" because they died at the hands of another.

As noted above, for the gun prohibition lobby, of course, this is also "gun violence." Nobody tags suicide by hanging as "rope violence" or leaping from a highway overpass as "bridge violence" yet the final result is just as terminal.

This may be a subject best discussed with a philosophy professor, but there is ample reason to include the subject here because it is part of the "big picture" of numbers games that the gun control crowd loves to play.

The wrong targets

Earlier, we alluded to the *Washington Post* Fact Checker piece that referred to research about the various sources of firearms used by armed criminals. The majority of those guns are obtained "on the street" or via theft – more than 47 percent – while 39.5 percent were obtained from "family or friends." In criminal transactions, a friend or acquaintance may have a gun that he sells or trades to another criminal for use in the commission of a crime.

For the record, all of these transactions are done without the benefit of a background check, and none of them would be even slightly impaired by a so-called "universal background check" (UBC).

Use the recent experience in Colorado, which adopted a UBC statute in 2013. According to the University of Colorado's *Daily Camera*, from July through November of that year, after background checks became required on all private firearms transactions, the state Department of Public Safety reported 4,792 such checks on private gun sales. Of that number, only 72 sales were blocked because of a criminal records problem. That amounts to less than two percent, and it does not mean that the would-be buyer ended up with no gun. He or she simply didn't get a firearm through legitimate means.

With statistics like this, it is no wonder that a nationwide Reason-Rube survey found that 63 percent of Americans do not believe that more restrictive gun laws will prevent criminals from obtaining firearms. That poll, released in December 2012, suggested that people with more education have higher expectations that gun laws will work, and women are more likely to believe this than men.

Fewer Republicans than Democrats believe additional gun laws will keep criminals disarmed, according to Reason. The survey was conducted by Princeton Survey Research Associates International and had a +/- 3.7 percent margin of error.

Significantly, the lowest probability of all gun sources is that the firearm comes from a gun show. This is not the first time research has identified gun shows as the least probable gun source for criminals, yet gun prohibitionists repeatedly ignore the data.

In 1997, the Bureau of Justice Statistics issued a report titled "Survey of Inmates in State and Federal Correctional Facilities: Firearms Use by Offenders" that found "approximately 203,300 prisoners serving a sentence in a State or Federal prison in 1997 were armed" at the time they committed the crime that put them behind bars.

The most revealing part of that report was a small table that showed fewer than one percent of these inmates got their firearms from a gun show (0.7%). When the report was revised in 2002 under the byline of Caroline Wolf Harlow, Ph.D., a BJS statistician, the figures were unchanged.

Another revelation was that "fewer than 1 in 50 State and Federal inmates used, carried, or possessed a military-style semiautomatic gun or a fully automatic gun during their current offense."

This tends to belie claims by gun prohibitionists that gun shows need to be heavily regulated, and that so-called "assault weapons" should be banned in order to reduce gun-related crime. If anything, the report suggests that these gun control strategies are essentially doomed to failure if reducing violent crime is the goal.

But, of course, that is not the goal at all and it never was, and the gun prohibitionists know it.

In reality, anti-gunners wish to have bragging rights to banning a whole class of firearms, and being responsible for imposing harsh restrictions on gun shows – i.e. background checks on every transaction, whether commercial or private – and forcing private citizens into background checks even if they merely lend a firearm to a friend, or trade one to a shooting or hunting buddy.

The added bureaucratic hoops are not designed to prevent criminals from getting firearms, but to discourage law-abiding citizens from buying, selling, trading, gifting or lending guns to one another; that is, they are adopted in order to prevent as many citizens as possible from exercising their constitutionally-protected civil right to keep and bear arms.

So, why do anti-gunners claim that these restrictions will reduce crime? Quite simply, it is a canard, and if not that, it is a delusion. Either way, it is not the truth, and there may be something more sinister at work.

As noted by conservative columnist Charles Krauthammer more than 15 years ago when discussing the ban on semi-automatic rifles under the Clinton administration, "...the assault weapons ban will have no significant effect either on the crime rate or on personal security...Its only real justification is not to reduce crime but to desensitize the public to the regulation of weapons in preparation for their ultimate confiscation."

If the public is made to feel comfortable about the ban of a whole class of firearms, and then another and another, ultimately the public will see no threat to the complete ban on firearms, and the confiscation – with force if necessary – of guns from people who do not cooperate.

Historian and researcher Clayton Cramer, writing in early 2013 dug up a quote from Pete Shields, founder of Handgun Control, Inc., which became the Brady Campaign to Prevent Gun Violence. Shields was quoted in a 1976 interview with Richard Harris, a reporter with *The New Yorker*, when he stated, "We're going to have to take one step at a time, and the first step is necessarily — given the political realities — going to be very modest. . . . [W]e'll have to start working again to strengthen that law, and then again to strengthen the next law, and maybe again and again. Right now, though, we'd be satisfied not with half a loaf but with a slice. Our ultimate goal — total control of handguns in the United States — is going to take time. . . . The first problem is to slow down the number of handguns being produced and sold in this country. The second problem is to get handguns registered. The final problem is to make possession of all handguns and all handgun ammunition-except for the military, police, licensed security guards, licensed sporting clubs, and licensed gun collectors-totally illegal."

Shields seemed to overlook the fact that this is the United States, not a police state. But if one looks at the more extremist gun control proponents, one will discover that they are not terribly concerned with the civil rights of gun owners. Their fear and dislike of firearms justifies, in their minds, their hatred of the people who own them, and makes it acceptable to use whatever means necessary to achieve an end that strips gun owners of their civil rights. And what does this hate translate to? Social bigotry of the worst kind; something akin to the blind hatred of blacks or Jews or Hispanics, though one will never persuade anti-gunners to admit it because above all else, the die-hard anti-gunner is too arrogant to admit they may be just as prejudiced as the worst racist.

The worst liars lie to themselves, which evidently makes it easier to lie to everyone else.

Straight from Page 11

Chicago Mayor Rahm Emanuel, who is credited with telling the world that "You never let a serious crisis go to waste; and what I mean by that it's an opportunity to do things you think you could not do before" appears to have taken an entire page out of the gun control playbook – Page 11 to be precise. According to the *Chicago Tribune*, he "used public appearances in support of his plan to cast aside research in favor of emotion, contending cost-benefit analyses provide little comfort to the victims of gun violence."

The two "key messaging principles" in a discussion of pressing "the toll taken by gun violence" listed on Page 11 are:

1. "Always start with the pain and anguish that gun violence brings into people's lives."

2. "Use statistics to reinforce an emotional argument, not to replace it."

This is a follow-up to the principle expounded on Page 6 of the anti-gun guide:

"Always focus on emotional and value-driven arguments about gun violence, not the political food fight in Washington or wonky statistics."

At least he sticks to the script. Recall what Joseph Goebbels, the Nazi propagandist, observed:

"The most brilliant propagandist technique will yield no success unless one fundamental principle is borne in mind constantly - it must confine itself to a few points and repeat them over and over."

Emanuel could hardly be compared to a monster like Goebbels, and it is never helpful when those in the firearms community equate anti-gunners to Adolph Hitler or his henchmen. But, to one degree or another, political propaganda is used on a daily basis by everyone in politics, whether on the left or the right, to sell their agenda, and Emanuel, who presides over one of the most violent cities in North America, where the *Chicago Sun-Times* maintains a running body count of homicide victims, is a true believer in citizen disarmament. His years with the Clinton and Obama administrations gave him plenty of opportunity and experience, but when he succeeded Richard Daley as Chicago's mayor, the gloves, and brakes, really came off.

One strategy he pushed, however, appears to have been stolen not from the anti-gun strategy guide but from the gun rights community: tougher sentencing for people who illegally possess firearms.

Emanuel's proposal would lock up armed criminals for at least three years and require them to serve at least 85 percent of their time behind bars.

That's a philosophy born in the "Hard Time for Armed Crime" and "Project Exile" programs championed by the Citizens Committee for the Right to Keep and Bear Arms and the National Rifle Association. When those two organizations backed getting tough on armed criminals, liberal pundits and people from Emanuel's far left corner of the political galaxy excoriated the notions.

Whatever else this demonstrates, it confirms that the anti-gun far left suffers from a world-class case of hypocrisy that keeps silent when something the firearms community has advocated suddenly proves to be the right approach.

Nearly one year after NRA's Wayne LaPierre observed – in the wake of the Sandy Hook attack – that "the only thing that stops a bad guy with a gun is a good guy with a gun," graphic evidence came in the form of Arapahoe High School gunman Karl Halverson Pierson in December 2013. He entered the school, located in the Denver suburb of Centennial, with a 12-gauge pump shotgun one day before the first anniversary of Sandy Hook, looking for a specific teacher who courageously tried to draw him away from the building by leaving.

Instead, Pierson cowardly fired a shot point blank at 17-year-old Claire Esther Davis, for no known reason. Miss Davis, an attractive and promising student, was hit in the face. She tragically died a few days later.

Pierson ran into a room near the library and, realizing he was being pursued by a sheriff's deputy who was the school's resource officer – and carrying a gun – took his own life rather than confront the lawman, "a good guy with a gun."

There will be many questions about Pierson, and for good reason. He was described as a dedicated student, rather than some quiet loner; a young man who had been on the school's debate team and had obviously not been in any trouble because he legally purchased the shotgun one week before the attack. To do that, he had to clear a criminal background check.

One other thing about Pierson that the mainstream press quickly overlooked because it did not fit the popular narrative is that he was outspokenly anti-gun. The *New York Daily News* and *Denver Post* reported a passage on Pierson's Facebook page that raised eyebrows: "The Republican Party: Health Care: Let 'em Die, Climate Change: Let 'em Die, Gun Violence: Let 'em Die, Women's Rights: Let 'em Die, More War: Let 'em Die. Is this really the side you want to be on?"

Following the attack, when the gun prohibition lobby realized that it was a shotgun that Pierson used rather than a so-called "assault rifle" – same as happened in the Washington, D.C. Navy Yard attack a couple of months before – instead of concentrating on the firearm, they began questioning why an 18-year-old could legally purchase a gun. That is swampy ground, however, because one quickly gets into an argument about why 18-year-olds should be allowed to vote or serve in the military. The political left does not want to go there.

The fallback position is simple: Attack the NRA. One can find the strategy explained on Page 23 of the playbook:

"We need to make it clear that we're taking on the NRA because we are alarmed by the way it blocks effective efforts to end gun violence and advances dangerous laws and policies that put people at risk."

It is all the NRA's fault. The Big Lie.

Registration and confiscation

One of the major concerns in the firearms community about so-called "universal background checks" (UBCs) is that they would include +some form of gun registration. That is a subject which gun prohibitionists almost religiously avoid, as it would confirm the fears of gun owners.

But for the gun prohibition lobby to deny that registration would ultimately have to be a part of their UBC framework is either deliberately deceitful or self-delusional. Either way, gun control advocates habitually speak of the "paranoia" in the gun community about registration leading to confiscation. It's the ridicule component of their argument designed to make firearms rights activists look foolish.

Yet firearms historian Cramer deftly put this debate into its correct perspective when he wrote, "There is another difficulty with a national background check system: in every scheme that I can imagine, an inevitable result will be some sort of firearm registration...

"Many Americans are concerned that firearms registration will inevitably lead to some future confiscation," Cramer continued, "and you don't need to be paranoid to think that: the second director of Handgun Control Inc. (the organization that today is the Brady Campaign) said explicitly in a 1976

New Yorker interview that registration was one of the steps towards the long-term goal of confiscation. More recently, gun-control advocates speaking in favor of confiscation of existing, legally owned firearms demonstrate that this is not paranoia but reasonable concern."

The gun prohibition lobby not only has scholars like Cramer to contend with, their background check schemes have a credibility problem with rank-and-file law enforcement. In the spring of 2013, only a few months after Sandy Hook and during a time when Congress was debating various gun control measures as a response to that outrage, PoliceOne, an organization with some 400,000 registered members comprised of active duty and retired law enforcement professionals, conducted a survey that garnered some 15,000 responses.

Among the things this survey revealed was that 70 percent of the respondents do not support "the concept of a national database tracking all legal gun sales." Additionally, 79 percent did not think a federal law prohibiting private, non-dealer firearms transfers between individuals would reduce violent crime.

Seventy-one percent of the respondents were favorable or very favorable toward law enforcement leaders who said they would not enforce more restrictive gun laws in their jurisdictions. In Colorado and New York following adoption of restrictive gun laws by Democrat-controlled legislatures, sheriffs in those two states rather publicly announced they had no intention of enforcing the new laws on the grounds that they were ineffective, unenforceable and – in the opinion of the lawmen – unconstitutional.

By the same margin – 71 percent – respondents to the PoliceOne survey thought that a ban on the manufacture and sale of so-called "assault weapons" would have no effect on reducing violent crime. More than 95 percent believed a ban on magazines that hold more than ten rounds would have no impact on violent crime, either.

Another area where anti-gunners will run into trouble is the growing popularity of concealed carry by private citizens, which the gun ban lobby seriously wishes to curtail and roll back to a structure under which local police chiefs or other officials have broad discretion about issuing carry permits and licenses. In such jurisdictions, particularly in Northeast states including New Jersey, New York, Massachusetts and down into Maryland, it is very difficult and time consuming to get a permit and the application process is deliberately discouraging.

What do police think about this? According to the PoliceOne survey results, 91.3 percent of the officers who responded said they support concealed carry by private citizens who have not been convicted of a felony and/or not been deemed psychologically or medically incapable.

The survey also revealed that more than 76 percent of the officers support the idea of armed teachers in schools, with annual firearms qualification requirements and vetting; essentially the same process officers go through. "A good guy with a gun" does not necessarily have to wear a uniform and badge.

Eighty percent of the PoliceOne respondents – remember these are active duty or retired law enforcement professionals – think casualties would be reduced if there had been legally-armed citizens present during any of the recent mass shootings.

All of these survey results translate to significant opposition to the gun control agenda by people who might be expected to support strict controls on firearms and the people who own them.

Here's an example of the Big Lie: Every time you see a politician, and particularly a president, pandering some new gun control scheme on a stage using uniformed police officers as a backdrop, that's a blatant misrepresentation of law enforcement support where very little, if any such support exists. It is done for one purpose only, to fool the American public into believing that the gun control scheme has the support of rank-and-file cops.

It is the street cops who will be called upon to enforce such laws, not the ranking brass that would send them out on such missions.

CHAPTER 10

WITH ENEMIES LIKE THIS, WHO NEEDS FRIENDS?

When *The Day,* a newspaper in New London, Conn., editorialized that "Responsible gun owners should welcome reasonable regulations instead of reacting knee-jerk against any effort to control such horrendous tragedies as Sandy Hook," they could just as easily have said that "responsible citizens should welcome photo identification checks before voting, instead of reacting knee-jerk against legitimate efforts to prevent voter fraud."

Naturally, an anti-gunner thinks law-abiding firearms owners – who have committed no crimes – should welcome the opportunity to be treated like a criminal.

The authors of that editorial tried to rewrite history, and Supreme Court rulings in two landmark Second Amendment cases, when they contended, "This nation's forefathers may not have conceived a weapon so destructive as an AR-15, but they recognized that it was necessary for the security of a free state not to infringe on citizens' rights to keep and bear arms, as part of 'a well-regulated militia'."

The high court has twice made it clear that the Second Amendment right to keep and bear arms extends beyond any service in a militia, rather than limiting the right to people who belong to, say, the National Guard, which is a popular, albeit thoroughly discredited, interpretation of the amendment. That a surprising number of anti-gunners steadfastly cling to this belief demonstrates just how fanatical they are about treating the right to bear arms as a heavily-regulated privilege.

For whatever inexplicable reason, editorialists filling column inches for mainstream press icons including the *New York Times, Washington Post, Los Angeles Times, Chicago Tribune* and other general circulation newspapers serving metropolitan areas dominated by liberal politics seem to treat the Second Amendment as a bastard child in the Bill of Rights.

The Day justified its anti-rights position by insisting, "This newspaper has long championed tight but reasonable restrictions on the sale, ownership and operation of weapons, and sees no conflict in this position with the Second Amendment of the U.S. Constitution."

Of course not; elitists consistently fail to see any problem with trampling the rights of other people, so long as their own rights are not jeopardized, and they have no personal interest in the rights being sacrificed. While newspaper editorial writers are understandably absolutists about the First Amendment and freedom of the press, far too many adhere to the belief that the right to keep and bear arms is some sort of collectivist right of states to form militias, and that individual ownership of firearms should instead be heavily-regulated by the government.

These are the same kinds of people who often suggested in the past that only the police and military should have guns, but then rail about incidents in which police fatally shoot some criminal, complaining about excessive use of force and "police brutality." Yes, it makes perfect sense until they are challenged to explain just why it is they want to give a monopoly of force to the very people they accuse of excessive force.

It does not help when the people who champion such contradictory nonsense make it clear from the outset that they really do not know what they are talking about.

In *The Day* editorial, as so many other mainstream writers have done over the years, they erroneously identify the AR-15 as "high-powered, rapid-fire weapons." True, the semi-automatic commercial version of this modern sport-utility rifle (a fact that the newspaper scoffed) can empty a magazine fairly fast, but even law enforcement professionals have overwhelmingly rejected the notion – as confirmed by the *PoliceOne.com* survey mentioned previously. The results of that survey pose problems for anti-gunners, because it is hard for them to argue that police officers are wrong about efforts to ban such firearms.

This much can be confirmed by looking at statistics on firearm-related fatalities of law enforcement officers for 2013, the most recent year for which preliminary data was available from the National Law Enforcement Officers Memorial Fund. NLEOMF tracks officer fatalities and found that in 2013, there were 33 officer fatalities, down a significant 33 percent from the 49 who were killed the previous year.

Just as significant is the fact that of all those officers, only six were killed with any kind of rifle, and two more were killed with shotguns. The majority were killed with handguns.

But did the mainstream press report this? Newspapers like *The Day* will pontificate about the public's right to know, but when it comes to offering details that go against the popular narrative, the facts seem to evaporate with troubling regularity.

Writing for *Annenberg Digital News* (neontommy.com), Executive Producer Syuzanna Petrosyan engaged in a bit of advocacy journalism, noting, "the number of parents and relatives of victims from (2013) shootings can provide advocates with a ready mobilized group who would be more willing than others to act for the campaign, become the face of the campaigns, and more strongly influence decision makers."

"By engaging in an extremely targeted persuasion campaign," she counseled, "advocates can create more ambitious social change by using those who have been affected the most by the tragedies.

"In addition," she said, "there is an opportunity to reframe the gun-control debate and messaging, differentiating it from the past."

This advice is directly in line with the strategies outlined in the gun control playbook, although there is no indication that Petrosyan was relying on the document to frame her argument.

However, this does show that anti-gunners do think alike. "Start with people, not laws," the guide advises, just pages after it also suggests, "Always start with the pain and anguish that gun violence brings into people's lives."

But in her zeal to whip up the campaign against various forms of gun control, Petrosyan does something unintentionally that casts a huge shadow over one of the gun ban lobby's top agenda items: the so-called "universal background check."

"Since 1982," she wrote, "there have been at least 62 mass shootings across the country, which have included 30 states. Of the 143 guns possessed by the killers, more than three quarters were obtained legally, according to a *Mother Jones* investigation."

So much for background checks; if more than 75 percent of identified gunmen in mass shooting rampages were able to pass a background check, this suggests a rather ineffectual process that just might be considered a wholesale waste of time. Of course, no gun prohibitionist will ever acknowledge this probability. Instead, they simply demand even more invasive checks, ranging all the way up to mandatory character references for anyone buying a firearm, as is the case in some other countries.

Increasing numbers of people are seeing through the smoke and mirrors, and realizing that the kinds of arguments gun grabbers make have more holes than a brick of Swiss cheese.

This may never have better demonstrated than by the attack in Santa Barbara by Elliot Rodger on May 23, 2014. His rampage involved the fatal stabbing of three people and shooting three others, and the police investigation significantly revealed that California's restrictive gun laws, which anti-gunners have demanded elsewhere, didn't prevent the carnage.

Rodger had purchased three handguns, undergoing three separate background checks and three state-mandated waiting periods. Authorities found that he possessed only California-mandated ten-round magazines.

Here in a single horrible incident, three of the key ingredients in the overall gun control agenda failed miserably. Not only that, the case also demonstrated that people with violent intentions can carry out their evil acts with a weapon other than a firearm. Still, there is an emerging tendency by people to refer to this tragedy as the "Santa Barbara shooting" as if all the victims were shot. It may not be deliberate, but it is certainly dishonest.

But focusing back on Petrosyan, one thing she did note is something with which people in the gun rights community might agree, and that is the way she describes former New York Mayor Michael Bloomberg: He's a "gun control policy entrepreneur." That is a polite way of explaining that he's a billionaire who thinks all of his money gives him some right or authority to dictate how everyone else lives.

Let the experts speak

"Mainstream" journalists are not so eager to talk about the experts who suggest there may be at least a partial solution to all of the mass shootings she laments. According to Terry Nichols, an assistant director at Texas State University's Advance Law Enforcement Rapid Response Training (ALERRT) Center, private citizens could be the answer.

According to the *Washington Times* and *Yahoo News*, "Almost half of the active shootings are over before additional help can arrive," quoting a study published by the FBI Law Enforcement Bulletin. Perhaps most significant, the study said "potential victims actually stopped the attacker in 17 such cases," the newspaper noted.

Yahoo News quoted Nicholls, who observed, "This tells us that citizens and bystanders have a very real and active role in stopping these events. If we can properly prepare and educate civilians, maybe we can get to where 90 percent are stopped by civilians long before the police arrive."

Nicholls is an ex-police officer, so one might think his opinion – despite its departure from the popular anti-gun narrative – would be appreciated.

Or how about Detroit Police Chief James Craig? He has certainly gone through something of an epiphany about guns in the hands of private citizens, and concealed carry, since beginning his law enforcement career in California. He went to Maine, where he found himself faced with issuing carry permits in a state that is across the country, and perhaps across the universe, from his former home. There, he found stacks of carry permit applications on his desk and he realized that he simply could not sit on them.

He discovered, according to a profile in the *Detroit News,* that legally-armed, law-abiding citizens do not create problems for police, and they actually provide a deterrent to criminals.

"Coming from California, where it takes an act of Congress to get a concealed weapon permit," he was quoted as stating, "I got to Maine, where they give out lots of CCWs (carrying concealed weapon permits), and I had a stack of CCW permits I was denying; that was my orientation.

"I changed my orientation real quick," he explained to reporters. "Maine is one of the safest places in America. Clearly, suspects knew that good Americans were armed."

Craig also made some comments during his time in Cincinnati, Ohio, that suggested that he still held some anti-gun bias toward so-called "assault weapons," but what he told reporters in Detroit raised eyebrows. Days later, in an on-air interview with the Fox and Friends morning news program, the chief reiterated his beliefs about private gun ownership.

Those views brought a reaction from Robyn Thomas, director of the Law Center to Prevent Gun Violence in San Francisco.

"I think at its core, his position is an emotional one, based on the idea that people feel safer when they have guns. But studies have shown more guns don't deter crime," Thomas told the *Detroit News.* "There's no research that shows guns make anyone safer, and it does show that, the more guns in any situation, the higher the likelihood of them harming either the owner, or people who have access to them."

By no small coincidence, on page 15 of the gun control playbook, there's a point/counter-point discussion on how to respond to the suggestion put forth by Chief Craig. The gun control guide advises readers to argue, "There's not a shred of credible evidence that more guns and more shooting save people's lives. More guns and more shooting mean more tragedy."

But, wait a minute. That's not really accurate, unless one subscribes to the notion that any evidence rebutting the traditional gun control talking points is "not credible," and that appears to be the case; i.e. "Disagree with me and you are not credible."

There actually are some genuine studies that do suggest more guns in private hands deter crime, and they have not been refuted. A study done by Mark Gius, an economist at Quinnipiac University, suggested that, "Using data for the period 1980 to 2009 and controlling for state and year fixed effects, the results of the present study suggest that states with restrictions on the carrying of concealed weapons had higher gun-related murder rates than other states. It also found that assault weapons bans did not significantly affect murder rates at the state level."

And Thomas obviously overlooks the famous research by Prof. John Lott, published as More Guns = Less Crime, the ground-breaking book that challenged the accepted dogma that widespread gun ownership and use were responsible for America's violent crime. Lott's book set the anti-gun movement on its ear, infuriating gun control advocates.

Lott's work has been summarily dismissed by anti-gunners, but as conservative columnist Ann Coulter noted in a discussion of Lott's work, "Unable to produce a single peer-reviewed study to discredit Lott's conclusions, while dozens of studies keep confirming them, liberals have turned to their preferred method of simply sneering at Lott and neurotically attaching 'discredited' to his name. No actual discrediting ever takes place. But liberals think as long as they smirk enough, their work is done."

In other words, when all else fails, resort to name-calling, or simply allege that someone's work has been "discredited." The same thing was attempted with Gius in the days after his paper was released.

When this level of disingenuous discourse has been reached, simply dismissing arguments favoring gun rights and using firearms for personal protection and then moving on – as in getting away from a losing argument – is a tack often taken by gun prohibitionists. Muddy the water or simply get out of it altogether. Or they might just begin spewing ridiculous arguments that have no foundation in fact. In the *Seattle Times* when readers began debating new White House gun control suggestions in early 2013 dealing with mental health records access, one reader offered the ridiculous assertion that following the Sandy Hook attack, "The gun lobby supported armed encampments at our schools to avoid a tyrannical over reach of the executive branch…"

Another chimed in with this remark: "The gun-nut lobby will make up any lie they can to prevent any sensible legislation to protect the public from gun violence, including rules that would help to uphold current laws preventing mentally unstable people from obtaining guns.

"How far we have come in the debate from the 70s when the NRA urged gun control legislation because the Black Panthers wanted a few shot guns of their own. Perhaps today we need an assemblage of mullahs in robes and turbans to parade the streets of Dallas TX, proudly supporting their 2nd amendment rights, their legally obtained weapon of choice in full view."

That's right, play the race card; accusing one's opponent of being a racist is a favorite ploy of the liberal, as it distracts the audience and deflects the argument into a realm where holier-than-thou creates a smokescreen.

In Rhode Island, a reader of the *Providence Journal* expressed delight that new gun laws were driving gun-related businesses out of Colorado. She had this to say, "Let the owners of murder wholesale be chased from one state to another. Until no state says yes to the kind of weaponry that let Adam Lanza slaughter a whole classroom in seconds."

Another gun control supporter, this one writing to the *Salem Statesman-Journal* in Oregon, observed, "Citizens' arms today are not a militia, but an outright population danger. Newtown, Conn. parents who have lost children due to violent gunshots and many more unfortunate parents could form a class action lawsuit before the Supreme Court against the Second Amendment…"

Nothing like having a rational discussion, eh?

Flunking the 'smell test'

The gun control guides counsel anti-gun activists to focus on emotions, using statistics only to bolster their arguments. Unfortunately, those statistics frequently go unchallenged.

For example, the *Poughkeepsie Journal* published a report noting, "Nationally, 617 children 14 or under died in unintentional shootings between 2001 and 2010, according to the National Center for Injury Prevention and Control. Most of the victims – 513 – were boys."

Break out the pocket calculator and divide 617 by ten, the number of years in the timespan mentioned by the newspaper. That's 61.7 fatalities a year, certainly not a good number, but nowhere near as alarming as it was intended to be.

By comparison, according to Safe Kids, a website maintained by the Northeast Georgia Medical Center with funding from the Medical Center Foundation's Healthy Journey Campaign, "Since 1999, an average of more than 815 children ages 14 and under have died as a result of unintentional drowning each year."

The website also reveals that "Drowning is the third leading cause of unintentional injury-related death among children ages 14 and under."

Translation: More children aged 14 and under die in a single year from drowning than die from gunshot wounds in a ten-year period.

To quote the playbook, "Statistics, properly used, can be a powerful way to make people understand the human reach and impact of gun violence in America..." As we discussed in the previous chapter, it depends upon how one defines "gun violence" and what data is pushed under that umbrella term.

Perhaps the 815 children who drown annually are victims of "water violence."

Of course, 617 childhood deaths related to firearms mishaps is no laughing matter, and firearms owners understand that many things can be done to reduce that number. However, with anti-gun resistance to such common-sense gun safety programs as the National Rifle Association's Eddie Eagle project, or firearms safety training as part of the public school curriculum, it's not an easy job.

When former Congresswoman Gabrielle "Gabby" Giffords and her husband, former astronaut Mark Kelly, traveled to Olympia, Wash. in January 2014 to testify in support of a gun control measure, Kelly told the House Judiciary Committee that in the years from 2001 to 2010 there were 5,692 gun-related deaths in Washington. It was an impressive figure, until someone did some basic division to learn that amounted to just over 569 fatalities annually. How many of them were suicides and accidents rather than criminal homicides? Kelly was not around to answer.

When ABC broadcast a special about children and guns headlined "Young Guns: A Diane Sawyer Special," she and reporter David Muir discussed some interesting numbers. In 2010, the report said, 98 "American kids under age 18" died in accidental shootings. That same year, 1,337 "American kids under age 18" died from gunshot wounds.

However, that same year, according to the Centers for Disease Control, "seven teens ages 16 to 19 died every day from motor vehicle injuries." The CDC reported that in 2010, "about 2,700 teens in the United States aged 16–19 were killed and almost 282,000 were treated and released from emergency departments for injuries suffered in motor-vehicle crashes."

One is compelled to wonder how many of those teen gun-related deaths were connected to gang activity.

Sawyer and Muir were heavily criticized by the firearms community for what was considered disingenuous use of data to create an impression that was simply not accurate.

Still, it remains far easier for anti-gunners to launch an emotion-driven campaign to hype their cause *du jour*, gain some headlines and have their moment of fame in the spotlight to, if nothing else, maintain some sort of relevancy.

Working with people whose civil rights you openly want to trample in order to achieve some common good is not only difficult, it can be embarrassing, especially if a goal of reduced criminal violence or accidental firearms deaths is achieved without penalizing law-abiding gun owners who did nothing wrong in the first place.

The Poughkeepsie newspaper reported at the time that the Moms Demand Action for Gun Sense in America – an organization that joined forces with Michael Bloomberg's Mayors Against Illegal Guns in early 2013 – would be pushing so-called "safe storage" proposals in several states.

This is nothing new. Indeed, such proposals have been part of the gun control agenda for many years, and every time one of these agenda items is resurrected, it reminds gun rights advocates and lawmakers how stale the anti-gun wish list has become. With each new high profile crime, the gun ban crowd dusts off this stale list of talking points and tries to convince lawmakers and the public that adoption of their package is a way to prevent future crimes.

The National Shooting Sports Foundation (NSSF) has for several years operated "Project ChildSafe," under which it has given away more than 36 million gun locks. NSSF also provides information to people about gun safes, locking steel gun cabinets and other security devices, but for many in the gun control crowd, this still is not good enough.

What they want is a mandatory law that requires gun owners to do this or that, essentially treating them as would-be criminals. For the most rabid anti-gunners, this amounts to "just punishment" for anyone who would dare to have a firearm in the home, and it also constitutes a "trophy" on the mantle of gun control; a victory, as it were, to wave in fund raising appeals and at luncheons or dinners where more checks are written.

Foot-in-mouth disease

On more than one occasion, gun control proponents have let slip a remark that – if caught by an alert reporter or editor – could lead to an embarrassing series of questions about motives regarding gun control goals.

For example, in a discussion regarding the paper that appeared in the *New Haven Register*, done by Mark Gius, the economics professor at Quinnipiac University, a Connecticut gun grabber named Ron Pinciaro, executive director for Connecticut Against Gun Violence (did you ever notice how all of these organizations pick names that give the impression their groups represent broad portions of the population when in reality they represent a small but vocal minority of anti-rights extremists) acknowledged, "Most gun homicides are committed in urban centers and they're not committed with assault weapons."

Remember the data we discussed previously about rifles and shotguns used in homicides? The newspaper should have asked Pinciaro why, after that admission, his group wants to ban semi-automatic rifles? After all, if they are not used in many crimes, where is the problem with their ownership by law-abiding private citizens?

There can be no other logical explanation than the most obvious, mentioned previously. Gun prohibitionists are not interested in reducing crime nearly as much as they want to ban guns, one type at a time if necessary. Such a ban is a trophy, and they take it very hard when a ban is prevented or struck down.

One example was the reaction to a federal court ruling in Illinois that nullified a ban on the selling of firearms in the City of Chicago. This prohibition was inserted into the city's gun regulations that were crafted after the 2010 Supreme Court ruling in *McDonald* v. *City of Chicago* that ended the Windy City's 30-year ban on handguns.

Anti-gun Mayor Rahm Emanuel publicly stated that he strongly disagreed with the ruling by District Court Judge Edmond E. Chang, an Obama appointee. He was quoted in the press insisting, "We need stronger gun safety laws, not increased access to firearms within the city."

But leave it to the Moms Demand Action group in Illinois to lament that it was "shocked that in a densely populated city struggling to keep children safe from gunfire, the court has dealt a serious blow to public safety by essentially encouraging more citizens to arm themselves."

A quick reaction from the blog Gun Free Zone that observed, "When you insinuate that your fellow citizens of a particular locale are too stupid/dumb/untrustworthy and/or as criminal as violent felons, you might be insulting them and counterproductive to your cause.

"On second thought," the blog added sarcastically, "go ahead and keep doing it."

Following the landmark *McDonald* ruling in a case brought against the city's handgun ban by the Second Amendment Foundation, Chicago under then-Mayor Richard Daley rushed into law the most restrictive handgun ordinance it could conceive. It required training just to get a handgun permit to keep a gun in the home inside the city limits, while at the same time prohibiting the operation of gun ranges anywhere in the city, where that training could be accomplished.

SAF went right back to the federal court with *Ezell* v. *City of Chicago*, and beat the city a second time. The court ruling explained that just because someone could probably travel to a gun range outside the city to take a course and shoot a firearm, such a scenario was ridiculous. One cannot claim to enforce a civil right by telling someone that they can exercise that right elsewhere, the court noted.

While anti-gun extremist organizations are a nearly-constant source of gaffes, newspaper editorial pages can be gold mines of easily-refuted information and comments that are so demonstrably false that one is astonished the editorials make it past the fact checkers.

Witness an editorial that appeared in the *Daily Olympian*, a newspaper published in Olympia, Wash. This editorial dealt with two competing citizen initiatives to the state legislature, I-594, an 18-page gun control measure disguised as a so-called "universal background check" proposal, and I-591, a one-page counter-measure supported by a grassroots coalition of gun rights, hunting and law enforcement professionals.

Falling quickly back on what has become something of a bad habit for anti-gun editorial writers, the article in question twice alluded to the National Rifle Association in such a way as to create the impression that the NRA was behind I-591. That intimation was absolutely false, but no matter, it makes good copy to use the NRA as a bogeyman whenever supporting an erosive gun control measure.

"Initiative 591 would prohibit expanding the background check requirements unless a uniform national standard is adopted," the editorial accurately noted. "It would also prevent the state from confiscating firearms without due process, which is an NRA-fueled red herring scare tactic."

Not so for anyone who remembers the aftermath of Hurricane Katrina, where more than 1,100 firearms were seized without warrants or probable cause, or anything remotely resembling due process. The outrage spawned a book called *The Great New Orleans Gun Grab*. It took a federal lawsuit filed jointly by the NRA and the Second Amendment Foundation to stop those confiscations.

The point, of course, was to demonize the NRA and make it sound like the organization was acting out of paranoia, when in truth, the NRA had nothing at all to do with the wording of the measure. Indeed, several days after the editorial appeared, an NRA representative, testifying before the state Senate Law & Justice Committee, confirmed that the organization had not taken a position on I-591, yet did anyone in the mainstream press report that? Of course not.

Later in the editorial, the *Daily Olympian* said this: "(W)e aren't looking forward to a highly charged emotional campaign funded by the NRA and other outside interests that has the potential to turn nasty."

At the time the editorial was published, the NRA had not contributed a penny to the campaign effort but ironically, the Mayors Against Illegal Guns organization founded by Michael Bloomberg had just contributed $30,000 to the gun control initiative effort. Based in New York, MAIG apparently was not the "outside interest" that the editorial writer had in mind when writing the hit piece. The hypocrisy, however, was not lost on *Daily Olympian* readers, left comments like this:

"What idiot on the editorial board wrote this POS?"

"This article is trash."

"Do you do ANY research into these things? Do you have any documentation or proof to show the NRA contributing to I-591 or do you just make the assumption, 'hey, it has to do with guns so the NRA has to be behind it'."

Likewise, far too many in the media cling to the notion that the 2008 *Heller* ruling by the Supreme Court "gave" something when it affirmed that the Second Amendment protects a fundamental individual civil right to keep and bear arms.

For decades, anti-gun media pundits have erroneously subscribed to the theory that the Second Amendment was written to allow states to form militias, the so-called "collective right" theory that is such rubbish even Supreme Court Justice Antonin Scalia, when he authored the *Heller* ruling, dismissed it out of hand.

Yet, Francis Wilkinson, a member of the *Bloomberg View* editorial board, was compelled to write the following as part of a short essay on a string of gun control defeats for the City of Chicago: "Gun-rights activists won the sanction of the U.S. Supreme Court in 2008, when an individual right to possess firearms was established for the first time (something the National Rifle Association had long feared testing in court)."

Second Amendment scholars would argue that the individual right "was established" when the U.S. Constitution, and the Bill of Rights, was ratified more than 200 years ago.

However, one thing Mr. Wilkinson did note accurately was that "Gun sales have reached record levels during President Barack Obama's presidency, with 2013 proving to be another banner year."

Indeed, Mr. Obama and other anti-gunners have only themselves to blame for increased gun sales. When they venture anywhere close to the gun issue, firearms and ammunition sales spike. More people apply for concealed carry permits and licenses. There is increased attendance at gun shows and more traffic at commercial gun ranges. It is not a stretch of credulity to hold that the firearms industry is one of the Obama administration's rare private industry success stories, and that goes double because his administration did not spend millions of taxpayer dollars on an industry that went broke.

Because of the push for gun control, demand for firearms and related products went up, and with that came additional jobs.

What happened at the state level is part of that, with some industries relocating from states that adopted restrictive gun laws to more gun-friendly and business-friendly states. Revenue lost to state coffers ended up in other states, along with the new jobs and improved employment data.

Another troublesome part of this broad campaign is best exemplified by California's "micro-stamping" law, passed in 2009 and fully implemented in 2014. This statute mandated that semiautomatic pistols marketed in California must feature micro-stamping technology, which forces gun makers to inscribe tiny serial numbers or some other identifying unique code either on the face of the firing pin or inside the firing chamber, or both places.

In theory, the empty cartridge cases ejected by such a gun would make it possible for investigators to track the gun, and its owner, if such cases were recovered at a crime scene. Yet, testing of the procedure was less than spectacular, and in early 2014, two major American firearms companies – Smith & Wesson and Sturm, Ruger – both announced they were not going to use microstamping and essentially were turning their backs on California markets and customers.

The CEOs of both companies actually submitted statements to the federal court in California on behalf of a lawsuit filed by the Second Amendment Foundation that challenged the statute. Other gun companies quietly took the same stance, while Glock attorneys filed an amicus curiae brief in support of the SAF lawsuit. The California law was curiously dubbed the "Unsafe Handgun Act."

There was no small amount of irony at the time because Smith & Wesson had, only a couple of months before, announced a major contract with a California law enforcement agency for its semi-auto pistols.

It may be of little import to many people, but micro-stamping, according to various experts, can be easily defeated with a small file and a few minutes' effort to deface or completely erase those tiny imprints. Others have quietly suggested that the actual microstamp wears down after rather minimal use of the gun, within 500 shots.

In the final analysis, it probably doesn't matter whether microstamping works to solve crimes or doesn't. It's the trophy that counts, not whether it turns out to be useful.

CHAPTER 11

WITH EVERY CIVIL RIGHT COMES... POPULARITY

Rabid gun prohibitionists have delivered over the years some good messages about keeping firearms out of the wrong hands, keeping children safe, preventing accidents and so forth, but they have yet to understand that their biggest obstacle to gun bans is one that cannot be overcome.

People actually like guns. They want them, for personal and family protection, for hunting and recreational shooting, as a hedge against a societal collapse and maybe just because they can have them. The number of gun owners is growing, despite claims to the contrary, and while they believe in holding people responsible for misuse of firearms, they are not going to allow their rights to be eroded in the cause of political correctness.

It's the one thing that the authors of *Preventing Gun Violence Through Effective Messaging* and *Voicing Our Values – To Curtail Gun Violence* cannot get around. You will never completely convince everyone to willingly submit to massive firearms regulation no matter how emotional your appeal becomes because at some point, at least some of the people are going to draw the proverbial line in the sand and resist.

They will not surrender that tool of self-defense and self-reliance. They will keep it close because they have realized that police never arrive in the nick of time. They will pass on that tool to their child or grandchild, at which point it takes on the mantle of family heirloom rather than being just a firearm.

For years, perhaps generations, citizens in many states were told that they really didn't want firearms and concealed carry laws because the polls said so. They were told by newspaper editorials and their own state legislators that it wasn't safe for them to be armed.

Eventually, the people woke up, and for the past two decades, they have been steadily restoring their gun rights, legislatively and legally, and at the top of their list have been concealed carry statutes. It is not simply an issue of personal protection, either. It also has something to do with liberty, as free people can keep and bear arms.

According to a report by *Newsmax.com*, "Nationwide, an estimated 8 million to 10 million citizens legally carry guns, a jump from about 20 years ago, when the figure was less than 1 million."

That isn't just significant, it is staggering. Had this phenomenon to do with anything other than firearms ownership and concealed carry, it would be the Page One headline, above the fold, every day for weeks. We are not talking about a proverbial "tidal wave" of interest, but a veritable tsunami in terms of public attitude toward firearms ownership and use.

It must cause shudders among gun prohibitionists to see updated figures and estimates of the number of legally-armed citizens who, while they may not carry every day, have gone to the trouble and expense of applying for and obtaining a carry permit or license.

One of the most telling cases that underscore the public's desire to be armed was found in California following a pair of 2014 Ninth Circuit Court of Appeals rulings that upended the arbitrary discretionary carry permit process that had been practiced for years by several county sheriffs. The cases were *Peruta* v. *San Diego County*, backed by the NRA, and *Richards* v. *Prieto*, filed by the Second Amendment Foundation.

After a three-judge panel ruled that the restrictive licensing scheme, which required concealed carry applicants to provide a "good cause" for a carry permit, was a Second Amendment violation, sheriffs adjusted to a "shall issue" system. During the two weeks that followed the ruling – which was challenged by anti-gun State Attorney General Kamala Harris – Fox News reported that more than 500 carry permit applications had been submitted just in Orange County alone.

While that case was playing out in federal court, two other strong examples of this newly-recovered freedom could be found in Wisconsin and Illinois, the last two states to adopt some form of concealed carry. In the months after Wisconsin Gov. Scott Walker signed concealed carry into law, Badger State residents flocked to apply for carry licenses. By October 2012, according to WISN news, more than 136,000 Wisconsinites had obtained carry licenses. That is hardly an indication that people think carrying personal defense firearms is a bad idea.

The WISN report quoted Attorney General J. B. Van Hollen, who observed, "We're not going to have problems in society when law-abiding citizens are permitted to carry concealed weapons under the law."

Anti-gunners were not convinced, and wanted access to the license database ostensibly to learn how many licensees were arrested. But Wisconsin lawmakers did the smart thing with their legislation when they made those files off limits for the sort of exploitation that has occurred in other venues where such data is available.

Wisconsin's surge may pale in comparison to that of neighboring Illinois, the last state to adopt a carry law – forced to do so by the Second Amendment Foundation's lawsuit called *Moore* v. *Madigan*, and the legislature there had to be dragged kicking and screaming by the federal courts to comply with the Second Amendment. A stalling veto effort by Gov. Pat Quinn only temporarily postponed the inevitable, and it took a veto override vote to open the doors.

Steadfast opposition from anti-gun politicians including Quinn and Chicago Mayor Rahm Emanuel and dire predictions from gun control extremists seemed to signal just how far out of touch they all were with the citizens. Even before the state police began accepting applications for carry permits, the agency predicted that as many as 400,000 applications would be submitted during the first 12 months of the law's effectiveness.

As with Wisconsin just to the north, Illinois residents were sending a message that they were no longer to be treated like children or second-class citizens. One Illinois news chain, *Sauk Valley Media*, picked up an Associated Press story that noted, "about 4,500 requests for concealed carry permits were submitted on the first day" that the state accepted applications. Leading up to the date when applications could be submitted by the public, firearms instructors could apply, bringing the number to more than 11,000 requests logged by the end of the first day, according to a spokeswoman for the Illinois State Police.

So much for the assertion that people didn't want to be in the "Wild West" as the numbers immediately told a different story. They put the lie to arguments that people do not want more guns in their communities. People may want fewer guns in the hands of criminals in their communities, but they do want more guns in the hands of law-abiding citizens, including their own hands.

Oklahoma's KOTV reported that in 2013, "more than 60,000 Oklahomans applied for a gun license." The station also said the state

Bureau of Investigation launched a new system that allowed users to submit license applications or renew their licenses on line.

Sixty-thousand license applications in one year in a single state says a great deal about the public's desire to be armed. It is a number that creates nothing but consternation among the ranks of gun control proponents because the more people they "lose to the dark side," the more difficult it becomes for them to successfully push their extremist "gun violence prevention" efforts, which translate to gun control, a fact about which increasing numbers of people are becoming aware.

In Washington State, 2013 saw more than 54,000 new concealed pistol licenses issued by the Department of Licensing law enforcement agencies. That year wrapped up with about 450,000 active Washington CPLs in circulation, which may surprise some people because the state is generally considered "blue" in its voting pattern for national office.

Actually, that is a misunderstanding because liberal Seattle, Everett, Bellingham, Olympia and Tacoma skew the numbers while the rest of the state is actually rather "red." It amounts to about one in ten adults being licensed to carry in a state of about seven million citizens.

Neighboring Oregon is another prime example of the social shift. A so-called "blue" state because its voting patterns are dominated by liberal Portland and Salem and other communities along the Willamette Valley, once one gets outside of those enclaves one finds a solid pro-gun population, especially when traveling east of the Cascade Mountains. Get down around Bend, Prineville, Pendleton or Hermiston and one is in what typically is called "gun country" despite efforts by some of the local progressives to suggest otherwise. These are sparsely populated regions where, in the event of an emergency, it might take an hour or more for a law enforcement response, and by that time, the trouble will be over and instead of stopping a crime, the authorities will be investigating what transpired.

In 2013, Oregonians armed up at a rather vigorous pace to the point that one newspaper seemed to lament that one in sixteen Beaver State citizens had a concealed carry license. A story that profiled one woman who had been shooting for about 2 ½ years and was "still improving" brought home the message that even Northwest women have become interested in shooting and defending themselves.

In Kansas, where the cow towns of Dodge City, Ellsworth, Abilene and Wichita are so often identified as hearts of the "Wild West" (they really weren't, outside of movie theaters), the *Kansas City Star* reported that 2013 saw "a huge increase" in applications for concealed carry permits, and offered a prediction that the surge would continue if more talk about gun control came from Congress. Half-again as many Kansans applied for carry permits that year than during 2012, and the newspaper suggested that "The uptick was driven by a push to tighten gun laws at the federal level and the December 2012 school shooting in Newtown, Conn."

Here, again, the citizens, by their own actions, demonstrated a public shift in attitudes about guns, although Kansas has always been a rather pro-gun state regardless how they felt about guns in Kansas City or in the halls of the state legislature.

Look at New Mexico. The number of concealed handgun licenses doubled in that state in 2013, according to KWES News, quoting figures from the state Department of Public Safety. As in Kansas and other states, firearms instructors credit the surge to attempts by state lawmakers to adopt more restrictive gun laws. This follows a pattern that has been long-standing. Whenever the public is advised that new gun restrictions may be on the horizon, people rush to gun stores and apply for carry licenses.

Another Associated Press report revealed that Utah, which is definitely a "red" state, issued a record number of concealed carry permits in 2013. Even though a percentage of those are issued to non-residents, it follows the nationwide trend.

And then there are the states where no permit is necessary to carry either concealed or openly. As Second Amendment scholar David Kopel noted in discussing this trend, where once the state of Vermont stood alone in the category of what is generically called "constitutional carry," it has been joined by Alaska, Arizona, Arkansas and Wyoming, the latter allowing carry without a permit by residents only. Gun rights activists would like to see more such states fall into the "constitutional carry" category, as they consider it nobody's business – and certainly not the government's business – if they are carrying firearms for personal protection in a peaceable manner.

Some credit *Heller, McDonald*

Some experts have credited the Supreme Court victories in *District of Columbia* v. *Dick Anthony Heller* (2008) and *McDonald* v. *City of Chicago* (2010) for at least part of the surge. The reasoning is rather simple: With these rulings, increasing numbers of Americans have realized they have the right rather than a government privilege to keep and bear arms, and they are exercising that right.

Certainly, that is not the only reason, but it is one of the reasons that many newly-minted gun owners have offered, along with a general concern about being able to defend themselves when a police response time may be lengthy.

Additionally, changes in state laws over the past two decades that have made it much easier for people to carry a defensive firearm have also become a contributing factor. Today in a majority of states, so-called "shall issue" laws that prevent local sheriffs and police chiefs from arbitrarily denying carry permits and licenses to anyone other than the elite, politically connected, and even political supporters have given law-abiding citizens an advantage over such demagoguery by some anti-gun law enforcement official.

The realization that owning guns is constitutionally protected may have accounted for something of an awakening for many Americans who grew up in very gun-restrictive states where owning firearms has become something of a major undertaking. The hoops through which citizens are forced to jump have been designed to discourage people and, they did.

Perhaps understandably, many people who grew up in restrictive regions such as New York, New Jersey, the lower New England states of Rhode Island, Connecticut and Massachusetts, and certainly Maryland or Illinois never understood firearms and how they are woven into the American fabric because they never owned one. For them, a gun was something carried either by the police or criminals, and everyone else was caught in between. It was a symbol of a violent subculture to which they did not belong, and certainly wanted nothing to do with.

However, in the wake of *Heller* and *McDonald*, public attitudes began changing. As increasing numbers of citizens began realizing the obstacles that have been created to gun ownership, in terms of time and expense, they have begun challenging the justifications for such rules. Political change comes slowly, and there are times when it has taken a court challenge, such as *Heller* and *McDonald*, and other cases including *Ezell* v. *City of Chicago* and the virtual companion cases of *Moore* v. *Madigan* and *Shepard* v. *Madigan* to knock holes in the anti-gun bureaucratic barricades. Citizens who realize they will no longer be treated like criminals, or arrogantly dismissed by police who pompously believed they were the only ones who had the skill and knowledge to safely handle firearms, have been flocking to obtain their licenses and permits, as noted earlier.

Another reason for such increases in concealed carry is more personal to many people. They want to feel safe on the streets in an environment where – thanks to liberal policies and soft judges – increasing numbers of recidivist criminals and people who should be institutionalized because of their mental conditions are preying on innocents.

In some cases, so-called "aggressive panhandling" has become robbery and assault. In other cases, those "assaults" have become murders. Random attacks by roving gangs of thugs, perhaps best illustrated by the dangerous "knock out game" practiced by punks who come up from behind and knock people out with vicious punches to the head, also alarm people into carrying firearms for their own protection. Some of these incidents have been fatal, and people know that, which offers yet another explanatory piece of the puzzle.

It is also plausible that some of these newly-armed citizens got permits as a result of increased pressure for new gun control measures following high-profile attacks at Sandy Hook Elementary in 2012 or the theater in Aurora, Colo.

Women are buying more guns, according to a report from a CBS affiliate in Dallas, Texas. A reporter did a story on the upscale Frisco Gun Club, for offering a Ladies' Night Special every Wednesday evening. The club's retail shop is loaded with items for women, who make up "roughly 20-percent" of the establishment's membership, the story detailed. Women buy guns for any number of reasons but primarily they do it for personal protection.

That's not an isolated case. In June 2014, the *Seattle Times* published an in-depth report on concealed carry in Washington State, noting that the number of concealed pistol licenses there had tripled between 2005 and 2012. Of the 457,000-plus CPLs in circulation at the time, more than 100,000 of them were held by women, better than a one-in-five margin. That figure seemed to stun the Times reporters, possibly because they cater to a "Seattle-centric" reading audience that votes more liberal than the rest of the state.

A publication called *The Inquisitr* noted in early 2014 that "Women gun owners are becoming a significant constituency in America." Quoting data from the National Shooting Sports Foundation, *The Inquisitr* said the number of women participants in the shooting sports has "steadily increased over the last decade." Another revelation came from CNN when it reported, "Almost 80 percent of gun retailers reported a rise in female customers in 2012, according to industry figures. In Florida, 22 percent of the concealed carry permits are held by women. In Texas, women hold 28 percent of concealed carry permits, up sharply over the past decade."

According to WKRG News, which serves Mobile, Alabama and Pensacola, Florida, "The demographics of gun owners are changing to include women. According to the latest statistics, the percentage of American women who own a firearm has nearly doubled since 2005—rising from 13% to 37%. Part of that 37% can be found every third Tuesday…at Styx River gun range in Baldwin County."

The station interviewed Stephanie Turner, identifying her as the chapter president of the Northwest Florida Well Armed Woman group. Members cover all age groups from 20 to 60, she explained and the primary goal of this group is teach the safe handling of firearms and understand them.

In Arizona, a program promoting sport shooting for women was launched in early 2014 and it doesn't even touch on personal protection, but rather shooting clay targets with shotguns. Not surprisingly, many women who get involved turn out to be pretty good clays shooters.

A Wyoming news agency, *County10.com*, noted that a former Riverton police captain and firearms instructor named Mark Stone had been filling up concealed carry classes "as fast as he announces them." Even in Wyoming, where carrying firearms or having one in the window rack of a pickup is rather common, people are arming up and new shooters are appearing all the time.

One novel approach to this was a Valentine's Day effort by gun shops in Texas to market hot pink Glock pistols, according to a story in *Bizpac Review*. In conjunction, the Rosenberg Police Department posted a public service announcement on its Facebook page that encouraged men to buy their ladies "the gift of safety."

The same story noted that an Indiana gun shop had been suggesting that men offer gift course in firearms safety to their loved one.

A "gun enthusiast" identified as Shannon Teal told ABC-57 News, "I think if you get the right type of woman, it would be romantic for her," the story said.

In New Hope, Minn., the WCCO morning show spent several days focusing on things to do for Valentine's Day, and one of the segments dealt with taking "your significant other" to the gun range for a shooting session. The date included time on the firing line and lessons in gun safety. It apparently filled up fast because there were only eight slots available, at $250 a pop.

Still, a decade ago, such a date idea might not have been suggested, much less promoted on a local television morning program.

Marketing to the demand

Even CNN took an in-depth look at the women-and-guns phenomenon, discussing how some gun companies are now offering firearms in colors that appeal to females, and that's not just limited to handguns. Rifles and shotguns are also in the mix.

For example, Mossberg is marketing a line of shotguns and rifles in a pink camo the company calls "Muddy Girl." They feature shorter stocks designed to fit smaller-framed shooters.

Remington has also produced shotguns and some rifle models for smaller shooters, and has never been sorry about it.

Taurus has been, for some years, offering handguns in different colors, and there have been a few models from Charter Arms as well.

European American Armory has a female-oriented department it calls Pavona Arms, featuring handguns with smaller grips and more easily-cycled actions.

Putting it bluntly, there are many reasons why more people are buying firearms and getting licensed to carry, and it is not possible to simply explain the phenomenon away as some fit of paranoia by right-wing white males. One may argue that it's an "empowerment thing" while another will counter that it's a "self-preservation thing." They would both be right.

Nothing puts a small woman on a level playing field with a larger aggressive man than a firearm and the skill to use it effectively should the need arise.

Local gun ranges often establish "Ladies' nights" or women's shooting leagues, thus removing what was once considered an "intimidation" barrier that had women shooting alongside usually better-skilled men. That may have been the perception more than the rule, as it turns out there are a lot of female shooters who are consistently better shooters than men, and one can confirm that by their scores.

This is hardly exploitation as some gun control fanatics might argue in an effort to color and shift the argument, but a serious surge of interest from women for a skill that makes them competitive in more ways than one. In many respects, women who become interested in shooting are often better students than men because they seem to approach the subject differently, with no preconceived notions about shooting from the hip, or being as accurate as *Dirty Harry* was in all of those movies. Author Workman was a certified firearms instructor for 30 years and personally observed this in classroom and range settings.

Once women get a firm grasp of this newfound skill, they hone it and with each visit to the range they improve. They also find that shooting is relaxing, challenging and in no small way educational because every new shooter learns something new with each range visit and each press of the trigger.

Valentine's Day romance and all the other fluff aside, there is no doubt that shooting and gun ownership is not merely a passing novelty.

Ask anyone who owns and operates a gun range, especially an indoor facility in the middle of an urban or suburban setting. Invariably they will report heavy use, especially during the fall, winter and early spring months when recreational activities are often confined to some indoor setting because of weather. Interest in advanced firearms courses and training, and various shooting leagues has contributed to the demand for more range time, and more such facilities. This is particularly true in northern tier states, from Washington and Oregon east to New England.

Many of these ranges offer "Family Nights" not only to satisfy a need for some family activity, but as smart business people, they realize that a new generation of shooters is out there, and they will become customers at some point, provided they have an enjoyable experience at the outset.

And don't forget the men. For a growing number of men who are involved in the shooting sports and in owning guns for personal and family protection, this is more than just an opportunity to burn up a couple of boxes of ammunition each week or each month. They are interested in improving their skills, for that "day they hope never comes" at which time they may need to rely on those developed skills to save their own lives or the lives of their families.

What does this mean?

What does this growing interest in firearms mean to the gun prohibition lobby? It is obvious from the existence of the gun control playbooks that anti-gunners realize their work is going to be more difficult, so they have gone to the extent of producing guides for conducting gun control campaigns with advice on using semantics and emotion to sway the masses. They have eager legions of volunteer activists, whose ultimate goal is to remove guns from society, or at least from private ownership, and short of that, making ownership so cumbersome as to discourage people from having guns. In the firearms community, such people are occasionally referred to as "useful idiots."

Assembling strategy books is no small undertaking, but for it to have become necessary strongly suggests that the gun control movement is taking their campaign to erode gun rights seriously more than ever through emotionalism, and that their primary targets are the same people who are becoming more interested in, and enthusiastic about, firearms ownership.

It also suggests that the gun banners have realized they may be in some trouble from a public relations perspective, as they are finding that the old arguments and strategies no longer work as well as they did a generation ago.

So, they have learned to couch their arguments in terms of family and child safety, and are teaching their activist volunteers to do likewise.

Making persuasive arguments based on emotion and half-truth can work, until and unless the audience begins to understand that it is not really their safety at issue, but their civil rights. While people are in the process of figuring this out, they're getting hammered by messages designed to appeal to their emotions above all else.

Arguably the most insidious of all the messages one finds in *Preventing Gun Violence Through Effective Messaging* may be this one, instructing gun control advocates to: "Be clear that we know how to protect people from gun violence, which makes failure to act inexcusable."

We know. Translation: We're smart, smarter than the gun-loving rubes who disagree with us.

The instruction adds that, "This isn't a situation where we don't know what to do or are stymied in the face of an intractable problem. We know what it would take to prevent so many people from dying or being injured by gun violence. But those steps aren't happening because of a failure of leadership."

This reads all too suspiciously like a campaign brochure intended to convince people that a change of leadership is necessary, and "we" are the leaders you're looking for, the leaders society needs to initiate the solutions – i.e. "what it would take" – to so-called "gun violence."

And the use of "we" as the core of their message can also subliminally suggest that the audience is part of the "we" making this a case of alleged common knowledge that is being overruled by toadies for the evil gun lobby.

Anti-gunners have also learned to reach out to organizations that, a generation ago, might not have considered involving themselves in the gun debate because it was somewhat out of their league. This includes parent-teacher associations, whose primary focus should be on education.

The most effective way to counter this is to belong to such organizations and when they begin to stray into areas where their leaders may want to tread – thus trampling on your firearms rights – challenge them. One gun rights advocate went so far as to suggest that these groups be reminded that gun owners living in the school district might feel compelled to organize opposition to special levy and bond issues.

Dr. Timothy Wheeler of Doctors for Responsible Gun Ownership, has frequently told audiences to watch for those "boundary violations" from family physicians. If they start asking about guns in the home and offer advice on that subject, remind them that they are crossing a line from medicine to politics. Unless the doctor also is a certified firearms instructor, that medical professional has no business lecturing or even discussing firearms safety at home or anywhere else with his or her patients.

A complaint to the state medical board might be in order in such cases.

When it comes to the clergy, gun owners in any congregation can and should take a grievance to the church board. Clerical groups have habitually mixed anti-gun politics with their spiritual endeavors. One finds these organizations more active in metropolitan areas.

The involvement of clergy in gun politics raises questions about challenging the tax status of a church, but over the years there has been more talk than action in that realm. Some gun owners have simply left their congregations, with or without an explanation to the pastor. At some point it would seem reasonable to challenge involvement of a church pastor in one of these efforts, and demand to know why any gun owner in their congregation should continue to contribute to the collection plate.

Newspaper readerships have diminished in many regions, and while there is no hard evidence that part of the reason for their declining readership is due to increasingly leftward-creeping editorial policies that support every manner of gun control to come along, there is anecdotal evidence that many readers have cancelled subscriptions rather than financially support publications that use the First Amendment to continually trample the Second.

Editorial boards seem all too often to lean left, and editorial decisions that go so far as to eliminate outdoors columns or at least limit them to coverage of such activities as fishing, hiking, cross-country skiing, bicycle riding and photography – while giving short shrift or total disregard to hunting – have cost their newspapers valuable readers, whether they choose to believe that or not, and many do not. They live with the delusion that they are right and the backwards bumpkins who may disagree with an anti-gun and/or anti-hunting editorial policy don't matter.

Admittedly, one person or even a dozen people cancelling their subscriptions may not even amount to a blip on the financial radar screen, but hundreds or even thousands of hunters and gun owners ending their subscriptions is going to be noticed. And it has been.

Gun owners can now get their news from other sources, whether it is cable news networks or a variety of sources available on-line. The result is still the same. Declining subscription bases results in declining advertising revenues, and that ultimately results in financial troubles for the press.

The important thing for readers to do when they cancel a subscription over a newspaper's continuing support for the erosion of their civil rights, either on the editorial page or in the news columns when only one side of a story is told, is to let the publisher know.

Indeed, that's what gun owners can do when they part ways with churches or school boards or any other group. Be public about it. Let the neighborhood know.

This is the difference between playbook politics and pocketbook politics.

Or, as has been part of the American lexicon for a couple of generations: Money talks and B.S. walks.

CHAPTER 12

IF AT FIRST YOU DON'T SUCCEED, CRY, CRY AGAIN

When the anti-gun Moms Demand Action (MDA) group demonstrated at the Seattle Public Library, calling for state legislation that would prohibit the carrying of firearms in public library buildings – despite the fact that such a measure might be unconstitutional under both the state and federal right to bear arms provisions – they claimed it was for their safety and that of their children.

This happened just days after Washington Gov. Jay Inslee, a liberal Democrat for whom MDA members voted out of reflex primarily because of the "D" next to his name, had announced a moratorium on capital punishment while he remained in office. There was no small amount of irony in this because every one of the nine people on Washington's Death Row at the time had been sent there for killing women and/or children.

But far be it for a good flock of liberal anti-gunners to launch a diatribe against a man who had just sent a message to every would-be murderer that they could kill and not worry about facing the ultimate penalty during his watch. It is far easier to campaign against the civil rights of law-abiding gun owners, including the growing number of women discussed in the previous chapter, and such an effort plays well under the guidelines put forth in the gun control playbooks.

What about the many women who use the public libraries in the evening? What about their safety as they go to and from their vehicles or to the nearest bus stop? The Pacific Northwest has rather long, dark winters and the sun goes down pretty early in the afternoon from November through the end of January. Members of the MDA group are fond of saying that if a gun law saves the life of just one child, it's worth the inconvenience.

It apparently does not occur to them that rape, robbery, assault or murder amounts to a considerable "inconvenience" to the victim.

In Chapter Seven, we discussed the case of George Zimmerman and Trayvon Martin, the 17-year-old African-American teen who was killed on Feb. 26, 2012.

Perhaps not remarkably, there was hardly the same race-driven outcry in February and March 2014 when another 17-year-old black teen's name was in the headlines in the Pacific Northwest, but this time because he was the suspect in the murder of a 54-year-old white man, David L. Peterson, in the Greenwood district of North Seattle.

Peterson was killed after the teenage gunman first attempted to rob him of his cellphone, but then walked away after the older man wrestled his phone away and kept it. As Peterson called 911 to report the crime, the suspect allegedly heard him, so he turned around, came back and shot Peterson once in the chest at point blank range, and then fled the scene, according to police reports and court documents. That teen was arrested six days later at Seattle-Tacoma International Airport as he waited at the gate to board an airplane for a flight to Atlanta, Georgia.

While the press, as noted earlier in this book, essentially decided George Zimmerman was guilty even before he had been charged with a crime, there was a noticeable silence regarding the guilt or innocence of the teen accused in the Peterson homicide.

Liberal hypocrisy covers lots of ground, as is evident by decisions by anti-gun urban municipal government officials to create regulations limiting or eliminating the ability of personnel managers to ask questions about a prospective job applicant's criminal history. If you are going to be collecting a public paycheck, they are not interested in learning whether you may be a convicted bank robber or embezzler.

However, try to exercise the constitutionally-protected civil right to keep and bear arms, and one is expected to cooperatively submit to a criminal background check that just might be more invasive if anti-gunners had their way. Mayors and members of the city governments in San Francisco and Seattle have adopted the "no check" policy for hiring while visibly supporting adoption of so-called "universal background checks" despite the fact that there is no evidence to support claims that such checks can prevent violent crimes.

Background checks have, indeed, prevented retail gun transactions with people who were disqualified, but that doesn't mean those people did not subsequently obtain firearms through illicit channels. Indeed, they usually did, but nobody in the gun prohibition movement would ever acknowledge that.

With prosecutions for attempted illegal gun purchases at an all-time low – make that virtually nil – over the past few years, it should come as no surprise that criminals who were turned down for a firearm transaction at a gun shop or gun show would eventually obtain a gun via some alternative method.

As briefly mentioned in Chapter Five's discussion of anti-gun hypocrisy, the Seattle "Job Assistance" ordinance ostensibly restricts how employers can request and use background check information. However, under the law, employers in the city cannot require that a job applicant put a checkmark in a box on an application form that reveals whether they have an arrest and/or conviction record. Seattle is not the only municipality to have such a law.

In San Francisco, the same "limited use" of criminal background checks was imposed in early 2014 under the "Fair Chance" ordinance. This measure requires firms employing 20 or more people to "limit the use of criminal history information," according to *Bloomberg Law*. This prohibition applies "until the entity determines that the individual's qualifications meet the requirements for the position or affordable housing unit," *Bloomberg Law* explained.

In addition to San Francisco and Seattle, the cities of Buffalo, N.Y., Newark, N.J. and Philadelphia, Pa., have all adopted similar language in their codes.

This "head-in-the-sand" philosophy seems to run rampant through liberal municipal governments. It is almost as though the people supporting such double standards believe that if they personally don't see it happening, or acknowledge that it happens, it doesn't really happen.

One supposes that's a nice way to live in denial, but at the end of the day, nothing has really been accomplished.

Don't kid yourself that this sort of double-standard is limited to local governments. Following the adoption of legalized marijuana laws in Colorado and Washington, the Federal Bureau of Investigation established a rather oddball and surprising precedent when it announced that it would not conduct background checks on people wanting to operate retail marijuana businesses. The FBI announced this after having actually conducted such checks on some people in Colorado.

What was strange about this is that officials in Washington state had been pleading with the FBI for more than a year to come up with some kind of process to check the backgrounds of individuals wanting to set up pot businesses in the state.

The Associated Press did an expose on this situation, noting, "The Obama administration has said it wants the states to make sure pot revenue doesn't go to organized crime and that state marijuana industries don't become a cover for the trafficking of other illegal drugs. At the same time, it might be tough for the FBI to stomach conducting such background checks — essentially helping the states violate federal law."

What a shame the Obama administration didn't think along the same lines, or express the same concerns, when it was allowing the Bureau of Alcohol, Tobacco, Firearms and Explosives conduct, than cover up, Operation Fast and Furious, the gun running sting debacle.

There is one other important consideration in this case of dual standards. Nowhere in the Constitution will one find a delineated right to grow, smoke or trade in marijuana. However, the Bill of Rights contains that troubling old Second Amendment, which does specify that there is a right to keep and bear arms, and that it shall not be infringed.

Regardless of one's personal views on smoking pot, which remains a federally-designated "controlled substance" despite the Colorado and Washington laws to the contrary, if the Justice Department feels no necessity to conduct background checks on individuals who want to sell a product against which there are federal laws, then why should gun purchasers be subjected to such checks? It doesn't wash to argue "That's the law" when it comes to firearms, because the law in 48 states and the federal statutes still consider marijuana trafficking and use to be crimes.

The chosen ones

Then there are officials or celebrities ("public figures") who publicly speak in support of gun control, but privately own and even carry guns, themselves. Sometimes they argue that they are armed because of dangers – real or imagined – that somehow give them special dispensation to do what they tell others not to do.

These privileged individuals invariably consider themselves to be somehow above the fray, and entitled to extraordinary security when it comes to keeping themselves safe while they work tirelessly to deny the same opportunity to others.

Take the case of Dwayne Ferguson, the western New York activist who, according to the *Buffalo News*, "spent more than a decade advocating for nonviolence and peace in the streets of Buffalo."

However, in early 2014, Mr. Ferguson set off a chain of events that included a school lock-down that lasted for hours when he appeared at the Harvey Austin Elementary School armed with a handgun, for which he reportedly had a carry permit, according to the story that ran on WGRZ-TV.

He ended up being arrested and charged with two felonies.

As one might imagine, Ferguson's anti-gun supporters rushed to his defense. The Rev. James E. Giles, president of the Back to Basics Outreach Ministries, declared, "I'm sure Dwayne went into the school not thinking he had the gun on him."

Stop right there. Just how many people walk around carrying a firearm without knowing they are carrying a firearm? Veteran gun owners might suggest that anyone who is so scatterbrained that they do not know they have a loaded gun in a purse, briefcase, carry-on bag or piece of luggage, or in their pocket, just might want to reconsider owning a firearm.

Giles told a reporter that Ferguson even asked a police commander what the lockdown was all about, and when he learned it involved a report of a man with a gun, Ferguson apparently rounded up a bunch of youngsters and rushed them into the school cafeteria, then shut the doors.

More than ten years ago, the vocally anti-gun head of the Seattle Urban League got into trouble for having a gun in a school building, when he allegedly flashed the gun during a heated argument with another man. This happened at Rainer Beach High School.

James Kelly was the long-time head of the Urban League, an African-American who supported extremist gun control measures including the state's gun-free school zone law. Yet he had a state concealed pistol license.

At the time, Joe Waldron, a director of the Citizens Committee for the Right to Keep and Bear Arms, had this to say: "James Kelly obviously lives by the dual standard. He carries a gun for personal protection, while supporting laws that would deny others that same right. He allegedly carried that gun on school property, in violation of a law he supported, and reportedly flashed it to intimidate another man during an argument, violating yet another state gun law."

It took an inordinate amount of time for the Seattle City Attorney's office to charge Kelly, and many believe it was because of not only his race but his connections within the city's political elite circles. In the end, he agreed to perform 80 hours of community service to resolve the criminal charge, and he did not lose his CPL. He also issued an apology.

Or take the case of Illinois State Sen. Donne Trotter, a Chicago Democrat about whom CBS affiliate WBBM observed, "Trotter, 62, has been a state senator since 1993. Before that, he was a state representative from 1988 to 1993. During his time in the legislature, he has regularly been an anti-gun vote, and has opposed legislation that would allow for concealed carry in Illinois."

Trotter cosponsored more than 30 gun control bills during his legislative tenure. He also voted against the Illinois concealed carry law.

So, what was this opponent of concealed carry, this stalwart gun control supporter doing with a loaded .25-caliber semi-auto pistol in his carry-on bag? Trotter at the time was employed at least part time as a security guard, and an acquaintance suggested to a reporter that "it was an accident and he was employed by some security firm, and that could happen. If you're in a hurry, and you're getting off-duty, and you throw your gun in your case, you don't think about it. That can happen..."

The felony charge initially filed against Trotter was reduced to a misdemeanor. Trotter pleaded guilty and was sentenced to one year of court supervision and 60 hours of community service, during which time he said he would talk about "gun safety."

Fourth Amendment

Gun rights, as it turns out, is not just a Second Amendment issue. It is also a Fourth Amendment issue, at least when gun prohibitionists start meddling into the rights of gun owners.

The Fourth Amendment states, "The right of the people to be secure in their persons, houses, papers, and effects, against unreasonable searches and seizures, shall not be violated, and no Warrants shall issue, but upon probable cause, supported by Oath or affirmation, and particularly describing the place to be searched, and the persons or things to be seized."

Reacting to one of several gun control-related stories frequently published by the newspaper, one candid reader of the *Seattle Times* suggested that "unscheduled warrantless visits" by law enforcement to the homes of gun owners "Sounds like a good idea to me."

This followed a discussion in the newspaper that addressed firearms accidents in Washington State over the past two decades, but devolved into a debate about the relative merits of background checks and other gun control measures in terms of accident reduction. Of course, the answer is "no effect at all," because – as the saying goes – you cannot legislate against stupidity, and you cannot fix it, either. But that does not prevent extremist gun banners from continually trying, or at least contending that it might be possible with just one more law.

The question was posed to anti-gun liberals: How would they feel about unannounced, warrantless or no-knock searches by police, not acting on any criminal suspicion, visiting someone's home to determine whether they were growing marijuana in the basement? Remember, in Washington and Colorado, it is now legal to smoke pot recreationally. But the law does not allow anyone to be an unlicensed grower.

How about warrantless searches of someone's home computers to determine whether the owner had been cruising kiddie porn websites or using social media to set up encounters with minors?

The question was never answered. How could it be? The shoe was suddenly on the proverbial "other foot," and that foot was firmly inserted in the collective mouth of the anti-gun crowd.

Regulating gun owner privacy has always been addressed differently by gun control proponents than other privacy issues. The gun prohibition lobby has long engaged in perpetuation of the notion that it is everyone's business if there is a gun owner in the neighborhood, what kinds of guns that person owns, and how they are stored.

In actuality, that is nonsense. It is nobody's business what kinds of firearms a citizen owns, and certainly not the government's business, gun rights advocates would argue. If people are doing nothing illegal, or behaving irresponsibly with firearms, they ought to be left alone.

A couple of generations ago, such individuals were frequently referred to as "busybodies." This alluded to their habit of sticking their noses into everyone else's business, as though they were some self-appointed arbiter of public standards.

Such people evidently cannot be happy unless they are prying into the affairs of others.

Guided by advice in the gun control playbook, they justify this self-styled activism as "taking reasonable steps to keep dangerous weapons out of the hands of dangerous people."

Who determines what constitutes a "dangerous person?" In the minds of gun prohibitionists, anyone who owns a firearm for whatever reason – and especially those who are licensed to carry a concealed handgun for their personal protection – is a dangerous person. In the playbook, anti-gunners are advised that "Public spaces should be places where families can go freely and safely and not be overrun by unknown people carrying hidden, loaded guns."

Perhaps we should pause here for a show of hands. How many people have repeatedly carried loaded, concealed handguns in public places and have never been revealed to be armed? In other words, the armed citizen goes unnoticed, and thus never constituted a threat to anyone.

Truth be known, a lot of those families are protected by a mom or dad who happens to be discreetly carrying a loaded firearm.

This advice merely perpetuates the notion that the general public needs to be fearful of lawfully-armed citizens, even though these citizens go about their daily business without harming anyone. And the gun prohibition crowd has the gall to claim that armed citizens are paranoid.

There is one interesting point-counterpoint in the playbook that establishes yet another myth believed by anti-gunners.

The booklet points to one argument in favor of concealed carry reciprocity between the states. The pro-gun argument is stated thusly: "Congress should recognize that the right to self-defense does not end at state lines."

To counter this, anti-gunners are advised to suggest, "What about the right innocent people have to keep untrained, out-of-state people from carrying loaded, hidden guns into their communities?"

There is no such right spelled out anywhere for "innocent people." This "right" is made up from whole cloth. But the right of self-defense certainly exists, and it is recognized and affirmed with various state statutes that outline the use-of-force.

Perpetuation of this so-called "right" of "innocent people" is no doubt part of the fabric of rules and regulations established by local public housing authorities over the years. These rules have been successfully challenged by a series of legal actions involving the NRA, Second Amendment Foundation and the Citizens Committee for the Right to Keep and Bear Arms.

In March 2014, the NRA won a case against the Public Housing Authority in Wilmington, Del. The court overruled prohibitions on firearms in certain public areas of the housing project, and the reaction from the press was reported as "a surprising blow to public housing officials." But the report did not explain why this was a surprise, as it was not the first time a housing authority had lost a gun case.

In mid-2013, SAF won a similar challenge against the Warren County, Ill., Housing Authority. In 2009, a joint action by NRA and CCRKBA against the San Francisco Housing Authority was settled when the bureaucracy changed its rules about firearms.

Gun bans, or just overly restrictive gun regulations, in public housing are not allowed, period, end of story. That has been the consistent outcome of such cases, and equally consistent has been the reaction of bureaucracies on the losing side.

As the Delaware media coverage noted, "The ruling directly contradicts a July 2012 ruling by U.S. District Judge Leonard Stark who found that the limits on residents carrying guns in common areas like lounges, halls and laundry rooms was 'a reasonable policy'."

Housing Authority Executive Director Frederick S. Purnell was quoted stating his disappointment, observing, "Overall I think the ruling sets us back." Back from what? This was an unlawful prohibition as explained by the court, and if that forced the housing authority to step back from something, that "something" was probably even more egregious.

Purnell reportedly contended that restrictions on guns in common areas of the public housing project "struck a good balance between the right to bear arms and the overall mandate we have to provide a safe environment for our residents."

What's to balance? Where does it say the exercise of a civil right is somehow a threat to "a safe environment" for other housing authority residents?

One is compelled to suggest that this is the same mentality that has driven people to post their businesses as "gun-free zones" in the belief that erecting some invisible barrier to firearms is actually going to keep criminals out.

About the same time this happened in Delaware, the *Washington Times* was reporting that a bar in South Carolina was experiencing public backlash for having posted a sign in its window that not only banned firearms on the premises, but took the extra step of calling gun owners "losers" and "douchebags." The owner of that pub told the newspaper that he was a "conservative Democrat" who supports gun rights, "not the 'big-ass liberal' people are painting him to be."

Oh, sure; far better to be widely recognized as a foul-minded social bigot than a "big-ass liberal," right?

Underlying all of this appears to be an effort, whether deliberate or subconscious, to make the public increasingly uncomfortable about firearms in their proximity. That horse has already left the barn, however, because of the millions of gun owners across the nation who already legally carry firearms in public places. Depending upon the state, they have been doing so for several years, without leaving a trail of corpses in their wake.

It might be enlightening to delve into the number of man-hours involved in lawful concealed carry by the millions of citizens who do it on a regular basis, harming nobody in the process. Balance that against the number of mass shootings that have occurred in so-called "gun-free" zones.

That is the part of this political equation that gun prohibitionists haven't discussed and they dare not because the results would be devastating to their arguments.

Gun-free extremism

The notion of disarming the public in public places is redundantly declared to be "common sense gun safety," but for the ultimate exercise in gun-phobic extremism, one needs only look to the Oklahoma State Capitol in Oklahoma City.

In March 2014, when the annual visit of county sheriffs to the state legislature occurred, one unidentified lawmaker apparently complained about the firearms they were packing. That senator wanted the lawmen to leave their guns outside. That created a stink not only at the capitol, but across the internet.

Wagoner County Sheriff Bob Colbert told KTUL News, "Everybody in that building knew who we were. One of the senators, who they wouldn't tell us, complained because we were armed in the building. So we all packed up and left."

Forty sheriffs were involved in that decision, and they felt justifiably insulted.

This is a glaring example of just how childish anti-gunners can be. In many state capitol buildings, private citizens are allowed to carry firearms, and that includes openly-carried guns in some situations. In Olympia, Washington, for example, armed citizens have occasionally attended hearings visibly armed and state troopers standing by for security have not complained or tried to interfere. To date, nobody has been harassed nor have there been any incidents.

But when a lawmaker complains about armed sheriffs in uniform – which includes a belt and sidearm – that definitely pushes the envelope and sheriffs reacted accordingly. It also underscores the depth and childishness of anti-gun extremism, and just how far out of the mainstream gun prohibition fanatics have strayed.

There are other examples of true extremism in the anti-gun movement. Radio talk host Mike Malloy in Atlanta was criticizing a pro-gun measure in Georgia and during his diatribe, transcribed by *Newsbusters,* was the kind of thing that might just get a conservative talk host pushed off the air by the FCC.

Said Malloy, in part: "Jesus Christ! I would like to invite one of the NRA board members, and I'll be armed, let's just get this over with, OK? Come on down to Georgia and I'll be packing heat and you be packing heat or whether you want to or not, I don't give a damn, it's up to you. And you come, meet me someplace, and all of a sudden, see, we have stand your ground here, and all of a sudden I'm going to feel real goddamned threatened by you! And I will shoot you! If I feel threatened. The law says I can! Ha ha ha ha ha,ha ha ha ha ha!"

Imagine for just one moment if someone from the NRA or CCRKBA had responded with a "Bring it on!" That individual would be excoriated by liberal cable television talking heads, probably without context.

Then there was the flap over the way a workbook prepared for a middle school in Springfield, Illinois egregiously misrepresented the Second Amendment, and how it was defended by the school superintendent. According to the study guide's explanation about the Second Amendment, "This amendment states that people have the right to certain weapons, providing that they register them and they have not been in prison. The founding fathers included this amendment to prevent the United States from acting like the British who had tried to take weapons away from the colonists."

That bit of foolishness got national attention and was harshly criticized by former Judge Andrew Napolitano, senior legal analyst for Fox News, who observed that Superintendent Bob Hill was "making it worse by giving students in the suburbs around Chicago an inaccurate understanding of their rights."

The workbook language seemed deliberately aimed at giving students a false impression about their constitutional right to keep and bear arms. Judge Napolitano suggested it was indicative of a culture where gun restrictions were a way of life.

Clearly, the "cultural divide" that seems to be at the root of this hypocrisy is driven at least in part by the notion among gun prohibitionists that anything they do and any ideas they have are beyond reproach, while gun owners and Second Amendment advocates are consistently wrong and just as consistently deceitful.

Never mind that there is no conclusive evidence that a single restrictive gun law, be it a waiting period or background check, statutory gun-free zone or loss of gun rights for a criminal conviction has ever been known to have prevented a single violent crime or kept someone from getting a firearm when they should not have it.

Of course, anti-gunners will hear none of that. They are right, and will let you know it.

CHAPTER 13

FINISH THE JOB: TOOLS FOR FOOLS

When it comes to treating their own troops like foolish bumpkins who need to be micro-managed as they wage a war against the Second Amendment rights of their neighbors and fellow citizens, there is perhaps no better example of this endeavor than the Brady Campaign's on-line guide titled "Finish the Job."

It is a "tool kit" for like-minded drones who must be told how to write letters to editors and lawmakers, how to use social media to influence others, hold house parties where the banter will likely include some down-your-nose discussions of all the ignorant rubes who own guns, and so forth.

It may come as a news flash to the people who head the gun prohibition movement but these cut-and-paste-by-the-numbers guides and playbooks really do not change the landscape that much. The public is far less gullible than it was a decade ago, although big-money campaigns with slick advertising and deceptive messaging can still sway some people.

They encourage "their people" to contact their elected officials and policy makers, but to use an organization's pre-canned messages that carefully avoid sounding extreme by using terminology such as "gun safety," "common sense gun reform," and "universal background checks" that do not mention registration and possible future confiscation.

What this suggests is that these gun prohibition lobbying groups may actually be afraid to allow their neighborhood followers to write their own messages, since such personal messages just might reveal extremist positions, such as supporting outright gun bans, or classifying gun rights organizations as domestic terrorist groups.

Such messages could reveal their radical endgame, which is to nullify the Second Amendment.

We have chatted with various lawmakers and their aides over the years who unanimously say that such "flood the Inbox" campaigns do not influence them much, if at all. In some cases, the lawmaker and staff even get annoyed at this sort of lobbying effort because there is no guarantee that the sender is even one of their constituents. Besides, form letters are rather impersonal.

Personal letters and telephone calls get far more attention, and attendance at community town hall meetings, along with volunteering to support individual candidates only adds to the possible influence one might have with a lawmaker.

But the "Finish the Job" guide encourages community activists to "Mention your stake or role in the community," as though law-abiding gun owners have no such standing.

The guide also provides some advice on using Facebook, Twitter and other social media, with suggestions on people who should be "followed" on Twitter including Barack Obama, Joe Biden, Nancy Pelosi and other notable anti-gunners.

Admittedly, gun rights activists have not been quite so organized in their efforts, so as to produce playbooks or guides, but on the other hand, among them are some rather educated people who are tech savvy and can turn words into actions. More such folks are showing up all the time. For example, the gun rights community has been rather effective in organizing events, such as gun rights rallies during legislative sessions, and most of this organizing is done via the Internet.

Where this has been particularly effective is on various gun rights on-line forums – nearly all of which have political sub-forums where members may post notices and alerts – that allow word to spread quickly when there is an upcoming hearing or vote on a particular measure. Gun rights activists have been engaging in grassroots lobbying for many years, and the internet has made them even more aware. While they may not have public speaking skills, one thing they are able to do is turn out the numbers, especially for weekend events.

The Brady Campaign's "Finish the Job" guide is set up to concentrate on specific subjects, most notably the background check effort. And therein could be the biggest challenge of them all for gun owners. Then, again, maybe not.

Rasmussen, Gallup

There are strong indications that even with their playbooks and activism guides, gun prohibitionists are losing ground with the American public because their arguments are losing traction. A Gallup poll released in January 2014 – 13 months following Sandy Hook – revealed the highest public dislike for strict gun control since 2001.

Two months later, Rasmussen Reports released the results of its own survey, showing more likely voters oppose stronger gun control measures, with 53 percent of that poll's respondents turning thumbs down on tougher laws.

Most significantly of all was that the two surveys reported identical results when it came to public support for stronger gun laws and firearms policies. Only 40 percent of the respondents in either survey supported tougher gun laws.

Now, why is that? Speculation can run all over the political map, but in all likelihood, there are many reasons for increasing numbers of people to reject the gun control mantra as a solution. As noted earlier, the argument that such things as so-called "universal background checks," gun bans and magazine limits, will have an impact on violent crime and mass shootings is demonstrably false. Most of the mass shooters in recent years passed background checks and those who didn't either stole the guns they used – from people who had passed the checks – or obtained their guns through some other illicit transaction.

In the case of Kip Kinkel, the teen who opened fire at a high school in Springfield, Oregon, his father bought guns for him. He repaid both of his parents for their attempts to reach out to him by murdering them.

There is something else, and it is something of a conundrum for the gun control lobby.

In recent years, they have tended to acknowledge – albeit playing it down so as not to completely scuttle their efforts – that passage of additional gun laws will not guarantee to prevent all violent crime. Of course, gun prohibitionists have learned to insist that their gun control proposal du jour just might prevent a serious crime, and "if it saves just one life, it is worth it."

Translation: "We realize passage of this new proposed law is likely only to inconvenience law-abiding citizens and not impair some truly determined lunatic from committing mass mayhem, but we want you to support us anyway and if you don't we'll lay a guilt trip on you by insisting that the blood is on your hands, rather than on ours for trying to peddle a fraud."

Both the Gallup and Rasmussen polls reflected significant drops in support for gun control from the previous year. In the Rasmussen case, the shift was a whopping nine points, while the Gallup results signaled a seven-point shift. But factor in the time difference between the two polls; Gallup was taken in January and Rasmussen was taken in late March. A two-month time lapse between the two surveys just might have added an additional two-point drop to the Rasmussen data.

Despite this, gun control proponents remain devoted to citizen disarmament and have been pushing the same agenda with a tweak here or there for the past three decades. They have learned a lot in that time, what sells at a particular moment and what doesn't, and the various anti-gun strategy guides discussed in this volume can be adapted to fit particular issues, which could make them rather effective, except for the fact that they were created for social do-gooders who are not terribly well-versed on the subject of firearms, which may stem from the fact that they don't like guns and don't believe anyone should own one.

As the gun control playbook introduced in the first chapter stressed, this is a battle of emotions, in a war of attrition. Gun grabbers will keep coming back, hoping to wear down gun owners and Second Amendment advocates. One needn't be a firearms expert to wage an emotion-laden campaign against someone else's Second Amendment rights, one only needs to be able to arouse similar emotions in his or her audience, and incite activism. Forget about fact altogether seems to be the base strategy.

The strategy guides have provided "potting soil" as it were for local organizations to start their own campaigns and even put together short strategy guides, as was done by CeaseFire Oregon on its website "New Trajectory," which must have been named with what anti-gunners believe is tongue-in-cheek humor.

This short guide points users to sources where they can find "a collection of accounts by surviving family members for all sorts of shootings, including suicides." This link they have dubbed "Faces of Courage" and it was put together by Moms Demand Action for Gun Sense in America, an organization that melded with Mayors Against Illegal Guns in December 2013.

Next, the Oregon anti-gunners offer a resource on "Stories about Gun Violence," which was "put together by Barack Obama's organization,

Organizing for Action." If there is still anybody not willing to acknowledge that Mr. Obama is not a gun prohibitionist, please raise your hand.

CeaseFire Oregon promises in its message that "Stories about Gun Violence" includes video accounts; always good for stirring up emotions.

Another link on the website is "I Demand Action." This was put together by Mayors Against Illegal Guns, featuring "first-hand" accounts of "how gun violence has affected their lives."

Lastly, there is the sure-to-tug-at-the-heartstrings "How Long Will I Cry? Voices of Youth Violence." This section is "a collection of first-hand accounts of gun violence in Chicago put together by students from DePaul University," as if the violence in Chicago – where gun ownership is still heavily-regulated – somehow parallels crime in an Oregon community.

Of course, this sort of localized effort is hardly regional. It can pop up anywhere and is an example of the lengths at which gun prohibitionists will go to further their agenda, and when it comes to pushing an agenda, as noted earlier, the gun ban lobby has no intention of ever settling for anything less than the most restrictive laws they can pass.

Witness what happened in Albany, New York on the day that gun owners descended on the capitol to demonstrate against the state's infamous SAFE (Secure Ammunition and Firearms Enforcement) Act which banned so-called "assault weapons" and imposed an arbitrary cartridge limit of no more than seven rounds in a magazine.

On the day of the rally, the Associated Press reported that "Supporters of New York's gun control measures — among the most restrictive in the U.S. — held a smaller event inside the Statehouse to announce several new bills, including one that would prohibit anyone from buying more than one gun a month."

Anti-gunner Alex Dubroff, identified in the AP story as the head of an upstate New York chapter of Moms Demand Action for Gun Sense in America – the gun prohibition lobbying group that joined forces with Mayors Against Illegal Guns in December 2013 – summed it up when she said, "We are far from done." This was after anti-gunners managed to push through the SAFE Act! In addition to the one-gun-a-month proposal, there was also a gun safe or trigger lock requirement, and a ten-day waiting period on the delivery of all firearms.

Evidently, Ms. Dubroff forgot all about Dr. Martin Luther King's famous observation that "A right delayed is a right denied."

These people simply do not give up, and neither should gun owners interested in protecting their rights from what amounts to a wave of human termites. The gun control movement is determined to one day erase the Second Amendment from the Bill of Rights, and the national lexicon, and it has certainly ramped up that effort with user-guides on how to get it done.

Of course, polling data can bounce back and forth with each new outrage that was not stopped by the latest big-on-promises, small-on-results anti-gun-rights legislation, but for the fanatical anti-gunners who read the gun control playbooks, when their new fails to live up to expectations, they don't suggest a repeal, they just want to pass another new law.

In the process, they slip on their ballet shoes for another dance through the fresh blood spatters.

The Wizards of Ooze

Perhaps true to the press axiom that "if it bleeds, it leads," gun prohibitionists are constantly on the watch for any new tragedy they can exploit, thus bringing any or all of their gun control strategy guides off the shelves for another go-round.

This "blood dancing" can apparently be addictive, and now with text materials to shore up their talking points, some of the more outspoken – and successful – messengers of the gun control lobby are quite skilled at it. They might almost qualify for the title "wizards of ooze," which is by no means meant to be flattering.

After all, their stock in trade is not finding intelligent solutions to crime or punishing criminals. Their entire agenda is distortions that transfer guilt for violent crimes from the individuals who commit those crimes to millions of law-abiding American firearms owners who would never dream of breaking a law by deliberately causing harm to another person or their property.

Among the worst examples of this blood dancing have come from organizations that try to tailor their exploitation to local issues, such as the 2014 campaign to push so-called "universal background checks" in Washington state. Using the fatal Fort Hood shooting as a reason to urge people to attend a "campaign kickoff" event and promote their agenda via an e-mail just days after the incident, campaign organizers overlooked the fact that the gunman passed a background check.

If you are going to offer a solution to a problem, make sure it's a solution that has some semblance of relevance. Of course, blood dancers rarely make that distinction, hoping instead to tug at the emotional strings, or jerk the chains, of a public that may not pay much attention to details.

This is where all of the playbooks and guides fail. They are locked into a specific narrative that does not have much flexibility; that is, it does not appear much independent thinking is involved once the rhetoric is ramped up.

The gun control wish list since Sandy Hook has been topped by the ever-popular "universal background check," yet careful analysis of the handful of high-profile incidents that have occurred since then confirm that the alleged or confirmed shooters went through background checks because they bought guns at retail. None of them came from gun shows, nor were they purchased privately.

On the other hand, when convicted felons are arrested with guns, invariably they were obtained through illicit transactions, such as trading stolen firearms, in which none of the participants would have abided by a background check requirement.

None of this makes a whit of difference to gun prohibitionists.

If it is not "background checks," it will be some other item on their agenda. For example, they may wish to target "shall issue" concealed carry laws that allow very little discretion on the part of local law enforcement to deny a permit or license application from law-abiding citizens. To beef up their arguments, however, they may use examples of crimes committed by people who could not possibly qualify for carry permits, due to age or criminal history. They were carrying guns illegally.

These sorts of things pop up occasionally when there are stories involving teenage thugs engaging in drive-by shootings. Anti-gunners will offer the argument that "We need to tighten up on concealed carry licenses" as a remedy for teen criminals killing or maiming one another, which has nothing at all to do with lawful concealed carry. But don't try to confuse them with facts.

Let them do the confusing. Following the murder of a man at an Ohio bar, writer Phillip Morris launched a column in the *Cleveland Plain Dealer* that contained this paragraph:

"Let's challenge those in Congress that — as a *Plain Dealer* editorial succinctly stated Friday — continue to make it virtually impossible for the public to trace illegal gun ownership and the history of guns used in crimes."

Mr. Morris effectively launched a myth, or perhaps two. It is not impossible to trace guns that are illegally possessed by criminals once there has been an arrest and the guns are in police custody. It's not up to the "public" to trace those guns, but the police can do this with the Bureau of Alcohol, Tobacco, Firearms and Explosives rather quickly, provided that it is part of a legitimate, ongoing criminal investigation.

But the impression he creates is one designed to weaken existing federal law that prohibits "fishing expeditions" into gun tracing data, not to prevent crime but to provide information for possible civil lawsuits against gun makers and retailers. Anti-gunners have, for years, sought access to this sensitive gun trace data but the law stops them.

Witness how swiftly authorities were able to trace the origin of the shotgun used by Navy Yard shooter Aaron Alexis. If it were "virtually impossible" to trace guns, investigators would have been very slow to track that gun back to a Virginia sport shop.

Authorities were pretty quick to trace the gun used by alleged Fort Hood gunman Ivan Lopez. They had the information in a few hours. Ditto the pistols used by the Café Racer gunman Ian Stawicki in Seattle a few years ago, or the guns involved in the Aurora, Colorado movie theater attack, or the pistol used in the attack in Tucson that left former Congresswoman Gabrielle Giffords wounded and six others dead.

This notion that guns cannot be traced is so demonstrably untrue that it is a wonder why any responsible journalist would weave that impression into a story.

Yet, a few words here and there, either in a newspaper or in some fund-raising statement from a gun control lobbying group will essentially bamboozle the public into thinking the law much be changed. This is how gun control urban myths get started.

Another strategy the gun ban crowd will use is one in which they portray themselves as "willing to discuss" the issue of "gun violence." Writing in the Hartford Courant, Rand Richards Cooper insisted, "I am not interested in grabbing anyone's gun. Owning firearms is constitutionally protected, it is rooted deeply in this country's traditions and it is not going to go away. Surveys show this position accepted by the overwhelming majority of so-called 'gun grabbers' like me. The dark scenarios of government forces rounding up gun owners and seizing their weapons have no basis in our intentions."

But then he paints gun rights activists into the extremist corner of paranoid nut jobs.

"Can gun-rights defenders," he asks, "offer a reciprocal reassurance about their intentions? Is there a willingness to discuss trying to reduce gun-related injuries and deaths in this country? This question presupposes a prior question: Can we agree that 30,000 annual gun-related deaths (and many more injuries) is undesirable; that it is a problem? If we can agree on that, we can proceed to discuss how one might reduce these numbers without threatening the fundamental right to own a firearm."

Right in the middle of that sentence is another canard dealing with the number of gun-related deaths, and he knows it. This was discussed earlier. Of all the firearms deaths in the United States in any given year, the majority are suicides, not homicides. That's not a gun control issue; it is a mental health issue. There are, according to data mentioned earlier, between 12,000 and 13,000 actual homicides in this country annually, and of those, between 8,000 and 9,000 are committed with firearms.

But the myth of "30,000 annual gun-related deaths" is perpetuated once again, creating the impression we have that many murders.

Lastly, Cooper makes his side sound oh-so-reasonable by observing, as if it were an admission, "By no means am I suggesting that every measure proposed on my side is sensible. Some seem designed more for moral showboating than for practical results. I recognize that this truly is one issue for which the devil is in the details. But we won't even get to those details if we can't agree that the subject is worth talking about. Many gun owners view any such conversation as a Trojan horse designed to take their weapons away. Those on my side, meanwhile, view the refusal to enter into any conversation as a sign of rigid absolutism."

Having been at the table with gun prohibitionists a few times, the authors can offer some first-hand observations about their willingness to have a discussion. The "give and take" of such conversations typically runs along the lines of "You give and we take."

Gun prohibitionists rarely bring anything to the table other than lofty offers of "peace of mind." Ask them to agree to something serious, like shutting down a state pistol registry or making it less burdensome to obtain a concealed carry license, and they balk. There is absolutely no interest in serious negotiation. They already have something and they want something else, without giving up anything in the exchange.

Now, are Morris and Cooper dyed-in-the-wool extremist gun grabbers? Certainly not, but what they write is symbolic of the problem that exists, and this feeds the anti-gun effort. Second Amendment activists want to protect, and even restore, the gun rights that have been eroded over the past 100 years, while those who would willingly give up someone else's gun rights think it is extremism if gun owners cannot be cajoled to give up something for nothing.

Want to give fits to a gun grabber at the negotiation table? Suggest that in exchange for "universal background checks," you want national concealed carry reciprocity, or blanket recognition of what is called "constitutional carry," under which no license is required to carry openly or concealed in a peaceable manner, anywhere in the country, whether it is Billings, Montana or Buffalo, New York.

Tell a gun grabber that you might be willing to discuss one of their proposals in exchange for their willingness to talk about removing the requirements on gun owner registration and see how far that gets you.

Even if someone in the gun ban movement were to "agree in principle," they would spend the rest of their waking hours pressuring lawmakers to keep it from happening, and do it all behind the scenes so it would still appear they were negotiating "in good faith."

And to make that so, they would be out there in the ooze, arguing that if national reciprocity or "constitutional carry" were to become law, it would result in the streets running red with blood, especially the blood of innocent children.

'Common sense' or Nonsense?

Regardless of how simplistic, silly, invasive or downright hostile it happens to be, the mantra of gun prohibition is invariably couched in the context of "common sense." Whether prohibitionists preach gun registration, extensive background checks, longer waiting periods, training requirements, licensing for gun owners or bans on certain classes of firearms, be they handguns or so-called "assault rifles," anti-gunners uniformly deem any and all of these measures to be "common sense steps" toward gun safety. In the process, they deliberately reduce a fundamental, constitutionally-protected civil right to the level of a heavily-regulated government privilege.

You want 21st Century gun control? Attorney General Eric Holder told a House appropriations subcommittee in early April 2014 that the Justice Department had been exploring the viability of gun tracking technology. He revealed that this was among the ideas that were discussed in the gun control hysteria aftermath of Sandy Hook "when we were trying to get passed those common sense reforms."

And new restrictions are always portrayed as "reforms" and they are invariably "common sense." This selection of terminology is skillfully designed to create the impression that opponents of new gun laws lack "common sense" and oppose "reform."

But let's consider for a moment how practical Holder's so-called "common sense" approach might actually be. According to the article in the *Washington Free Beacon* that revealed the attorney general's strategy, the Justice Department wanted to spend a whopping $382.1 million on "gun safety" in fiscal 2014.

This included $2 million for "Gun Safety Technology" grants that – considering past Obama administration investments of taxpayer's money to bail out crony business endeavors by friends and supporters – would most likely never bear fruit. It would become wasted dollars that taxpayers would never see recovered.

President Obama also wanted $1.1 billion "to protect Americans from gun violence – including $182 million to support the president's 'Now is the Time' gun safety initiative," the news agency reported.

Spending lots of money on feel-good projects that accomplish nothing but create the impression that you are "doing something" is the high point of political charlatanism.

Among these alleged "common sense reforms" was consideration of an RFID-equipped bracelet that must be worn by someone in order to make a gun work. The *Free Beacon* also reported that, in addition to the idea about the bracelets, others were looking at GPS tracking devices to reveal if a firearm "moves away from the tracker, indicating the gun is lost or stolen."

If that sounds like an elaborate 21st Century electronic gun registration scheme, you're probably right, and it could actually evolve into much worse. If such encryption and coding were to become reality and thus a mandate, this would literally allow the government to monitor every move of every gun owner, where they hunt and when, their visits to the gun range, and their other movements as an armed citizen.

It is essentially a scheme by which gun owners would be wearing the equivalent of ankle bracelets, except on their wrists, like the Star of David tattoo, so they could be quickly and visually identified by anyone bent on practicing social bigotry.

And this is all proposed under the guise of "common sense." Not that these ideas came directly from Holder, but it would not be at all surprising to see him endorse such measures. Rest assured, if Eric Holder were to suddenly disappear from public life for whatever reason, there are many gun haters waiting to step into his shoes.

All of these suggestions are part of the "smart gun technology" campaign that has been an on-again, off-again effort for more than a decade. But the technology has never been satisfactorily proven to work 100 percent of the time.

The acid test for such firearms, according to many in the gun community, would be for the president's Secret Service security detail to carry and use them successfully for five or ten years before they would ever be recommended, much less mandated, for private citizens and local law enforcement.

These arguments fall on deaf ears within the gun control camp because their mission is to discourage people from owning firearms. The more difficult they can make the paperwork, and the more complicated they can force the products to be made, the happier they will be.

Yes, gun prohibitionists have suffered major setbacks. Two Supreme Court rulings and several lower court decisions guided by those rulings, plus expanded gun rights via laws adopted at the state level have compelled the anti-gun lobby to simply work harder.

The inference one gets from the title of the Brady Campaign's guide is that the "job" is not yet finished. It is the same thing one would presume by listening to Holder talk about the Obama administration's gun control proposals.

And retired Associate Justice John Paul Stevens, in his book *Six Amendments: How and Why We Should Change the Constitution*, provided more ammunition for anti-gunners. He suggested that the Second Amendment's delineation of the right to keep and bear arms should have an addendum after "shall not be infringed."

His suggestion: Add these five words "while serving in the militia."

Stevens was the dissenting voice on the *Heller* ruling in 2008 and he seems to have held a grudge for being on the losing side.

His arguments suggest a strained and rather myopic view of the Second Amendment, but his argument that it needs to be changed essentially amounts to an acknowledgement that the Bill of Rights tenet means what it says. So, it needs to be changed to say what he wants it to say.

The retired jurist, who was 93 at the time his book appeared, perhaps crystallized better than anyone what goes on in the mind of an anti-gunner with his pontifications about gun rights. Rather than see the right for what it is, and accept it, his philosophy is to see things as he would like them to be, and if they do not measure up, simply change the rules.

It's a variation on the old "take my ball and go home" approach.

What a sad and somewhat disturbing commentary on a former member of the highest court in the land that he would have such disdain for one-tenth of the Bill of Rights that he would advocate changing it. This was the document he took an oath to uphold the Constitution while using his best wisdom to interpret it as the Founders would have it interpreted, to uphold the rule of law.

For more than 200 years, the Constitution – including the Second Amendment – has stood as one of the greatest human documents. It has withstood the test of time and provided guideposts for where this nation should go as the Founders intended.

Suggesting that it is time to change the Second Amendment to suit some narrow view is not common sense, it is nonsense. Yet it is this kind of thinking that guides the gun grabbers, who are less interested in public safety than they are in parading some legislative trophy.

Whether they call themselves "the gun safety movement" or "gun reformers," or by any other deceptive title, they are gun rights prohibitionists and they know it. For organizations to assemble and publish what amounts to "user guides" for activists to undermine Second Amendment rights in their communities goes well beyond the "grass roots" level of activism.

These gun grabbers are well-financed, well-organized and they have lots of support from the dominant liberal press. Indeed, Michael Bloomberg's "re-structuring" of Mayors Against Illegal Guns and Moms Demand Action for Gun Sense in America as the $50 million "Everytown for Gun Safety" lobbying organization in Spring 2014 underscores the serious nature of these anti-rights activists.

Extremists do not engage in give-and-take, but only set out to take what they can away from the people they oppose. For them, it is their life's work, and they are ultra-zealous in their civil disarmament efforts.

For these hardcore gun prohibitionists, the job will never be done until they can remove gun rights from the American lexicon and turn the Second Amendment into an historic footnote.

Should that day ever come, rest assured that they will be dancing in the streets, oblivious to the blood of so many future crime victims who will have been unilaterally disarmed by foolish legislation pushed through by foolhardy politicians who have succumbed to the misguided rhetoric of fools.

Epilogue

DIRTY-DANCING TO EACH NEW TRAGEDY

Following the tragic slayings of six people in Isla Vista, the community near the campus of the University of California, Santa Barbara, in May 2014 it was not long before gun prohibitionists were trying to exploit the carnage, despite the fact that this case presented some serious hurdles for anti-gunners as we mentioned in Chapter Ten.

The multiple slayings committed by a 22-year-old narcissist included three fatal stabbings, plus the three individuals he fatally shot. Still, gun control proponents took pains to portray the incident as "gun violence."

Two weeks later, Shannon Watts, founder of the Moms Demand Action for Gun Sense in America – an organization financed by billionaire Michael Bloomberg as part of his $50 million so-called "grassroots" group "Everytown for Gun Safety" – did precisely that. Writing for the *Huffington Post*, Watts tried to exploit the incident as a "violence against women" event, despite the fact that only two of the six victims were women. She also portrayed the incident as a case of "gun violence."

"For too long," she wrote, "women have been left out of the discussion about gun violence."

Then, as if following the advice in the gun control playbooks, she steered her remarks toward emotion rather than substantive analysis.

"Clearly, the laws allowing our country's culture of gun violence are not being made by the mothers who lose eight children and teens every day to a gunshot," Watts wrote. "And yet, ironically, our weak federal and state gun laws disproportionately affect women. American women are 11 times more likely to be murdered with guns than women in other high-income countries. On average, 46 women are shot to death by a current or former husband or boyfriend every month. And those mass shootings that occur in America with startling regularity? Fifty-seven percent of them involve domestic violence."

176

Now, what's wrong with this narrative?

Santa Barbara was not a "mass shooting" so much as it was a murder spree and Watts knows it.

The closest Santa Barbara comes to "domestic violence" is the fact that among the victims were male roommates of the killer, and they were stabbed.

The killer apparently did not know either of the women he shot, and he certainly was not married to them or was a boyfriend of one or the other.

But gun prohibitionists like Watts had further troubles that they deftly tried to avoid. This slaughter occurred in California, a state that has adopted virtually the entire gun control agenda, including so-called "universal background checks," waiting periods and magazine capacity limits. The killer obeyed each one of these requirements.

He purchased three handguns, all semiautomatics, and passed three background checks.

He possessed 41 ten-round magazines, and was able to engage Santa Barbara County sheriff's deputies in two separate shootouts before crashing his car and taking his own life.

He did not have a California concealed carry permit and endured the waiting period and one-gun-a-month limit on handguns.

He did all of these things, and then he murdered six people. The crime literally ripped away any façade that the gun control agenda could, or would, prevent such a heinous crime. Yet gun control advocates continued to maintain that passing invasive background checks would somehow improve public safety and prevent people intent on committing violent crimes from getting their hands on firearms.

Is it any wonder why the gun prohibition lobby cannot gain traction unless it spends tens of millions of dollars on slick and deceptive messaging, aided by various playbooks and guides?

Billionaire Bloomberg can dig into his pocket and lay out millions of dollars for so-called "grassroots" political efforts, and attempt to buy elections that further erode the firearms and privacy rights of millions of Americans, but he cannot hide from the truth. Neither can any of his gun-grabbing contemporaries.

The hard edge of reality is this: Extremist gun control laws do not prevent violent crime, and they never will. There is no way short of divine clairvoyance for us to predict – and thus intervene – a violent attack that claims multiple victims.

There are a rare handful of incidents in which a mass killer has not purchased his murder weapons at retail and completed a background check or multiple checks. We have discussed these mass killings in this book, yet zealous gun prohibitionists cling to the self-delusion that one more restrictive law will somehow provide a panacea, or perhaps they simply want the rest of us to believe it.

If the real goal here is public disarmament, they should gin up the courage to admit it. But like they are irrationally afraid of guns, and the people who own them, and in many cases fearful of other things in life, the devoted gun prohibitionist is afraid to admit he or she wants to remove firearms from the landscape. These cowards would dictate to everyone else how to live, but first they must remove the tools of resistance.

Instead, they relish each new tragedy as an opportunity to exploit, so they can tie on their taps or ballet slippers and dance through the blood of the victims, using the gun control playbooks as their strategy guides, in the quest for gun prohibition.

There is little doubt that at some point, gun control proponents will figure out a way to call the Isla Vista tragedy a "school shooting," even though it did not occur on the campus of any school. It involved students at UC Santa Barbara, and that's hardly a qualification, but that sort of inconvenient fact has not stopped gun grabbers so far.

In the aftermath of any violent attack, there is an almost obligatory human demand that "someone has got to do something!" Unfortunately, the proposals that typically come from knee-jerk reactionaries are culled from a tired agenda that has been used and re-used so many times that the pages are worn. This agenda is patterned into each of the strategy guides discussed in this book.

Drive-by shooting involving juvenile gang bangers? We need to restrict concealed carry permits for adults.

Attack at a shopping mall? We need to enforce background checks on hunting companions before they can loan one another shotguns or rifles.

School shooting by someone who bought a gun from a retail outlet? We need to close the so-called "gun show loophole."

For some reason, the "solution" just never seems to fit the circumstances of the crime it is supposed to prevent. Gun prohibitionists know this, but they are convinced that any erosion of the Second Amendment is a good thing, and will one day produce the ultimate end result of a gun-free Utopian society.

Bloomberg's seemingly bottomless budget to bankroll the kinds of gun control programs he wants to foist on the nation – a nation that he would create in his image – does tilt the playing field. It also puts a lie to any notion that the "gun lobby" is invariably better financed than the disadvantaged activists who merely want their neighborhoods to be safer.

There can be no misunderstanding that the gun prohibition movement is willing to spend a fortune to erase the Second Amendment as a constitutional guarantee against infringement on the individual citizen's right to keep and bear arms. Anyone who allows himself to be lulled into a false sense of comfort that "they'll never take my guns" is living in denial.

Much can be learned by watching how today's gun control zealot operates according to the playbook. They move quickly to exploit a tragedy, relying heavily on emotion to dominate the debate, while avoiding serious factual engagement. Rather than answer a question directly because the answer may be too revealing, they shift the discussion.

Witness the discussion that occurred between radio talk host John Carlson, the popular conservative morning drive time personality at KVI in Seattle, and Nick Hanauer, the wealthy venture capitalist who largely bankrolled a gun control measure disguised as a "universal background check" initiative in Washington.

CARLSON: Do you think that more guns in the hands of law abiding people are a good thing or a bad thing?

HANAUER: Y'know, it depends on what you mean by a law abiding person. Was the guy in Florida who shot the dude for texting in the movie theater a law abiding citizen?

CARLSON: A former cop.

HANAUER: I mean, was it a good thing for that guy to bring that gun into that theater? Answer the question. Was it a good thing for that guy to bring that gun into that theater? Would you want to sit next to that guy?

CARLSON: The answer is no, but would 594 have changed that?

HANAUER: No, absolutely not. But you asked me a different question.

That is so disingenuous as to be laughable. Hanauer changed the subject, provided an answer to a question that he had not been asked, and then complained that Carlson hadn't asked the right question. But it is typical of the anti-gunner who does not wish to admit that his ultimate goal is public disarmament.

Unfortunately, this is how anti-gunners play the game, and they're getting better at it. Exploiting tragedy has never been beneath the gun

And be ready to say in public what they are doing: Dancing in blood; reprehensibly exploiting a tragedy to push an agenda of disarmament that will erode the rights and safety of honest citizens, and have no impact on criminals.

Once they've accomplished that, the only question that remains will be about which other civil right they will next begin waltzing into oblivion, because gun control is not just about guns, it is ultimately about control.

prohibition movement, and with at least three strategy guides to help them plan their moves, they have something of an advantage.

Still, a slowly growing number of people are getting wise to the fact that all of these gun control efforts and initiatives have a few things in common, not the least of which is the fact that none of them would have prevented the crime they are supposed to prevent, had they been in effect at the time.

In candid moments they will acknowledge this, with a quick caveat that "it's a reasonable step" toward something else. They never quite define what that "something else" happens to be, but it is never good for gun owners or their rights.

What can gun owners, and especially those who consider themselves activists, do about it?

You must do far more than sit at a keyboard day after day, pontificating to like-minded colleagues, complaining about the government and how your vote doesn't count (so why vote?), and then wonder why gun control legislation is passed, or businesses prohibit firearms on their premises.

Join a gun rights organization. There is force in numbers. Make certain that organization is aware of problems in your community or state, and that they do not simply allow those problems to exacerbate on the grounds that the battle is not winnable.

Contribute to local battles financially. Shooters are far too willing to spend $1,000 on a new gun, but are reticent when it comes to donating $50 to defeat an anti-gun initiative, or anti-gun candidate.

Support candidates who support gun rights. Let that be the acid test, not whether your union local or your mother or brother likes a politician or your dad always voted for one party.

Educate yourself, so that if you attend public meetings you can present informed arguments, and be seen as someone with a rational viewpoint, rather than a half-literate Neanderthal in dirty jeans or bib overalls and rubber boots. Those who can present good arguments and back up those arguments with data can be devastatingly effective against people who press emotional hot buttons.

And remember, the reason gun prohibitionists concentrate on tugging on emotional heartstrings is because the facts are not on their side.

In situations where anti-gunners try to shift the discussion away from the facts, call them on it. Don't be afraid to say, "That's not the question I asked, and you know it," because they do "know it." They are just hoping that nobody in the audience realizes it.

Notes

Notes